'A book writte   of
their career. It   e of
life and career   ing
alongside mar   ted
a rich treasur   nd
provides a sour   the
challenges of   eer
from different   the
conclusion and

                                  ies.
                                  Ltd.

'The book mal   her
less attention g   far
greater focus o   to
be true to you   rk.
The tools and   en
by career won   of
what they wri   d.'

                                  icy,
                                  nt

'Reflecting th   h,
Dent and H   or
women in th   er
steps throug   s a
practical too   es,
and constru   eir
working life

  Although   ill
find invalua   ill
allow them   nd
fairer for al   ly
read: it's a book to keep using over lifetime.'

– Tony Montes, *Senior Advisor for Talent Management
in ADCO UAE*

'The main lesson I have taken from reading this book is the importance of strategizing my own personal development. As a full time working mum I often put aside my own development needs, but these tools have given me the direction I needed to invest the time and focus to achieve the executive positon I am aiming for. The hints and tips given, in particular utilising the career coaching model, have been invaluable. Through the book, I realised the importance of taking ownership of my career and to have the confidence to challenge and understand the nuances of business development at senior levels. I feel now I have the tools and motivation to concentrate on my own career trajectory and balance work and home life by more productive means. I have been inspired to re-think my own coaching principles to relay onto my staff and I would highly recommend this book to any women who is currently career planning for senior roles.'

– Jo Di Cristofaro, *Regional Skills Manager, Ingeus*

'This book is excellent; it provides a great insight into others' experiences, as well as how they managed and adapted to those experiences. I'd recommend this to anyone thinking about their career – whether first, intermediary or final steps!'

– Nicola Denegri, *Senior Consultant,*
Kissing With Confidence Ltd

How to Thrive and Survive
as a Working Woman

How to Thrive and Survive as a Working Woman

The Coach-Yourself Toolkit

Fiona Elsa Dent and Viki Holton

Bloomsbury Information
An imprint of Bloomsbury Publishing Plc

B L O O M S B U R Y
LONDON · OXFORD · NEW YORK · NEW DELHI · SYDNEY

Bloomsbury Information

An imprint of Bloomsbury Publishing Plc

50 Bedford Square	1385 Broadway
London	New York
WC1B 3DP	NY 10018
UK	USA

www.bloomsbury.com

BLOOMSBURY and the Diana logo are trademarks of Bloomsbury Publishing Plc

First published 2016

British Library Cataloguing-in-Publication Data
A catalogue record for this book is available from the British Library.

ISBN: PB: 978-1-4729-3064-4
ePDF: 978-1-4729-2269-4
ePub: 978-1-4729-2268-7

Library of Congress Cataloging-in-Publication Data
A catalog record for this book is available from the Library of Congress.

Typeset by Deanta Global Publishing Services, Chennai, India
Printed and bound in Great Britain

Contents

About the authors

Fiona Elsa Dent is a management trainer, leadership coach, associate faculty at Ashridge, mother and grandmother. Fiona now has a portfolio career, having worked full time for more than thirty-five years. She was a faculty member at Ashridge for twenty-four years, and during her last ten years on the full-time staff held a role on the management team as director of executive education, in which she managed a faculty group and contributed to the strategic operation of the organization.

Fiona now enjoys a mixed portfolio of teaching, coaching, researching, writing and grandma duties. She still contributes to a variety of programmes at Ashridge, and also works for a range of clients as a management trainer and coach. She enjoys researching and writing, and since moving to a portfolio role has published two books in addition to this one. These are *The Leader's Guide to Managing People* and *The Leader's Guide to Coaching and Mentoring*, both with her co-author Mike Brent.

Viki Holton is a research fellow at Ashridge Executive Education, Hult International Business School. She has a degree in Psychology and is a regular speaker at international and national conferences such as the British Academy of Management. She was involved with the Ashridge Centre for Business and Society for over eight years, and her special interests currently are leadership, HR and influence, team coaching, and diversity, as well as issues around women's careers and women as leaders. Viki is on the editorial board of the journals *Gender in Management* and *Career Development International*. For a number of years, she was a member of the board of the European Women's Management Development network and editor of the network's newsletter.

In addition to research, Viki also enjoys writing. She has written many articles, book chapters and research reports, as well as an earlier book on women's careers written in partnership with Fiona, and she has co-authored a book on team coaching. In her personal life, Viki enjoys gardening, travel and occasional trips to Caithness.

Acknowledgements

Many people have contributed to the writing of this book, not least the women who have taken the time to tell us their stories – the 1,400+ women who completed our questionnaire and the women we interviewed. To all of them, a heartfelt thanks.

We also appreciated Kate Cooper at the Institute of Leadership and Management and Kate Kinninmont at Women in Film and TV, www.wftv.org.uk, for their support in circulating and promoting our survey within their networks.

We would also like to thank our colleagues at Ashridge, and in particular Jan Rabbetts, Carol Long, Sharon West and Mike Dell.

Introduction

Over recent years, we have worked with, and coached, a number of working women across many different sectors, jobs and levels. We hear many good stories about how things have improved for women at work, and there are still many 'firsts' where a woman has stepped into a role that had previously only ever been held by a man. However, it is also clear that women sometimes do not thrive and survive at work because of the challenges and barriers that they continue to face. There is not yet equality in every organization, and women's career opportunities and development are often not as good as for their male colleagues. This book offers a coaching toolkit to help overcome such problems – it is focused on the individual and essentially is about 'how to' be your own career coach!

So, let's take a look at some of the good news. For working women in the twenty-first century, things have never been better! There is no doubt that the opportunities and choices available to women have never been greater. Today (2015), there are some seriously impressive women in all walks of life – business, technology, politics, the voluntary sector, sport and the media, to name a few. Some examples of key appointments for which it is the first time a woman has held the role include:

- Chief medical officer – Professor Dame Sally Davies
- Chief executive of General Motors – Mary Barra
- Chief executive of the Crown Estate – Alison Nimmo
- Bishop of Gloucester – Rachel Treweek
- German chancellor – Angela Merkel
- Chief operating officer at Facebook – Sheryl Sandberg
- Chief executive of EasyJet – Carolyn McCall
- Managing director of the International Monetary Fund – Christine Lagarde

However, based on current research about working women, commentary in the media and general anecdotes, it is also true that these women, and others like them, remain a small, select group. It is also true to say that many women are on track already, and we believe that even they could take lessons from some of the ideas in this book. So, how can we help more women to fully achieve their career potential, fulfil their ambitions and have equality in the workplace? We believe that by being more strategic and organized about your career you could achieve more, realize your ambitions and, in general, have a more satisfying working life. We do, however, want to make it clear from the start that this book is not all about getting to the top and breaking glass ceilings; it is about **YOU** achieving your goals and dreams in whatever area you choose.

We offer ideas, tools and techniques to help readers to reflect, review, assess and plan for success and satisfaction in their working life. We define career success in the broadest possible terms, which for us means being satisfied, fulfilled and appreciated in whatever your career or work may be. We want this book to be useful for women at all levels in organizations, in any job and at any age or career stage.

We think the recipe for a successful and rewarding working life is finding a job you enjoy that suits your particular needs at your stage in life. To do this, it is beneficial to understand yourself fully, how you have travelled the route so far and what your future dreams and ambitions are in order to be able to make the right choices. Many women do not strategize and plan their career. This is a mistake – you need a plan. Not the sort of plan that is rigid and inflexible, but one that can be adapted and flexed as you progress. The plan gives you something to aim for rather than drifting aimlessly.

When we wrote our earlier book *Women in Business: Navigating Career Success*, we learnt from the women we interviewed and surveyed that there is still much to be done to ensure true equality for women in work. We also recognized that women have amazing talent and huge ambition, and are sometimes surprised by their own success. Many of the women in our previous research were already at middle and senior levels in their career, and talked a lot about what they could have done differently and earlier to achieve this success.

Based on feedback from the previous book, and at various events we have taken part in since its publication, women have indicated to us that there is a need for a practical and individually focused 'how to' book that will provide ideas, tools and techniques to help navigate the challenges and difficulties and to plan for a successful working life.

One of the biggest lessons we learnt from all the events and workshops and our current research is that sometimes women are so focused on doing a good job and proving themselves that they rarely take time out to reflect and think about their current situation, their achievements so far, and how they are going to develop, progress further and move forward.

This book is the result of these conversations, our research and our continued interest in helping to address the need to help women reach their true potential and take an equal role in society at every level. It is essentially about awareness and practical skills to help you understand and realize who you are, what you have achieved and how you can build on that.

And, for those of you who are content in your current role and workplace, we also think this book will be helpful to you. It's not solely about moving onwards and upwards – the insights offered will help you better understand your own values and belief systems so that when you do have to make decisions they are better informed.

Our key aim in writing this book is to provide ideas, tools and practical suggestions that will help any working woman to thrive and survive.

Chapter 1

Career audit

If women are to reach their full potential and become an even more power-ful force in the world, we believe that one area that will actively contribute to this is for women to adopt a more structured and strategic approach to career management. This involves being more planful, analytical, organ-ized and systematic in managing their career progress and path.

Our research has indicated that for many women, the process of planning and actively managing a career path proves to be a challenge. Many cite issues such as:

- no time to do this
- I will do it but not yet
- no point in doing this
- lucky to have a job
- lucky to be able to work part-time
- limited possibilities due to partner's career situation
- happy where I am
- I simply don't believe in making plans

In this chapter we will introduce you to processes for self-analysis and career audit. We will encourage you to examine and review your career so far by posing a range of questions. These questions will all be supported with practical exercises to assist your analysis and to help you explore your skills, capabilities, strengths, weaknesses, ambitions and dreams. The questions that will contribute to your analysis and audit are illus-trated in the model on the next page.

In order for any person to thrive and survive in today's complex and uncertain business environment, having good knowledge of yourself and an understanding of what you want from a career are prerequisites. This will help you navigate a path towards achieving ambitions and being prepared and confident enough to make and take opportunities as they arise. Lack of confidence and self-belief are huge challenges for women. Even Helen Mirren admitted to lack of confidence in a recent feature in

Self-analysis and career audit questions.

the magazine *Woman and Home*: 'I wish I'd told my younger self to be more confident.' And in the same feature classical violinist Nicola Benedetti said: 'I'd tell my younger self to read more, study more – and be more serious.' We know that one of the causes of this lack of confidence is a lack of awareness of current skills, strengths and capabilities as well as not appreciating what they have achieved so far in their lives and work. By conducting a structured review of these, women are often surprised by what they find out about themselves. Of course, the earlier you do this the better, but doing it at any age will undoubtedly be beneficial for your future.

In one workshop we ran at Ashridge, we encouraged the participants, who ranged in age from late 20s to mid-50s, to adopt an analytical approach to review their career. Many were pleasantly surprised by the knowledge they gained when they thought and talked about themselves and their career so far. In this chapter, we will take you through a similar process of analysis by posing the five self-analysis and career audit questions mentioned earlier. We will also suggest a range of practical reviews and exercises that will help you to learn more about yourself and will encourage you to think about your career future in a more confident and strategic way.

Before we begin the career audit, we suggest you complete a 'skills and qualities audit'. The purpose of this is to enable you to clarify and understand your strengths, weaknesses and development needs in a range of key skills. These skills and qualities have been selected to enable you to comprehensively review four key areas:

- personal skills and qualities
- relationship skills and qualities
- strategic skills and qualities
- career skills and qualities

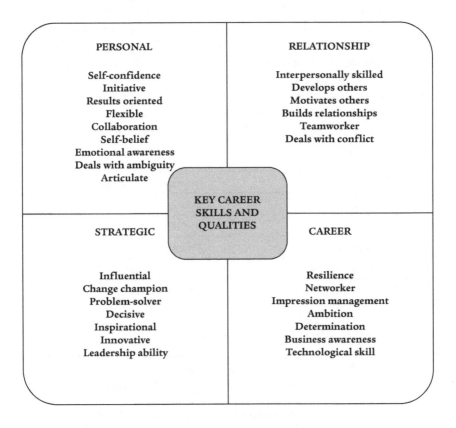

The skills and qualities have been selected based on what we hear from women when researching, coaching and teaching and in consulting assignments.

Skills and qualities audit

This audit takes the form of an inventory in which you can assess your own skill and ability in each of the twenty-nine skills or qualities. For each one, we will ask you to assess yourself in relation to two questions: first, how skilful you believe yourself to be, and secondly, how important the skill or quality is to your particular career situation. Not all of them are relevant or necessary for everyone. It will always depend upon your own career choice, situation, stage and personality.

The lists are by no means exhaustive; rather, they are a selection of what we have heard in our research and what we hear people talking about as those skills and qualities that contribute to their success in their career. Examine the audit and assess yourself on each of the skills or qualities. The measurement we are using is on a scale of 1 to 5, where 1 indicates low skill or low level of importance and 5 indicates expert-level skill and a vital level of importance. There is also a space to make any personal notes that you think may be useful for your analysis. The table below summarizes the descriptors for each level.

	Skill level	Importance rating
1	Unskilled	Unimportant
2	Some skill	Some importance
3	Average skill	Average importance
4	Above average skill	Very important
5	Expert	Vital importance

CAREER SKILLS AND QUALITIES AUDIT			
	Skill level (your current ability in this area) Score yourself 1–5	Importance rating (relevance to your particular career/ role) Score yourself 1–5	NOTES
PERSONAL SKILLS AND QUALITIES			
• Self-confidence • Initiative • Results oriented			

• Flexible • Collaborative • Self-belief • Emotional awareness • Deals with ambiguity • Articulate			
RELATIONSHIP SKILLS AND QUALITIES			
• Interpersonal skill • Develops others • Motivates others • Builds relationships • Teamworker • Deals with conflict			
STRATEGIC SKILLS AND QUALITIES			
• Influential • Change champion • Problem-solver • Decisive • Inspirational • Innovative • Leadership ability			
CAREER SKILLS AND QUALITIES			
• Resilience • Networker • Impression management • Ambition • Determination • Business awareness • Technical skill			
YOUR OWN IDEAS			

Use the space below to make notes about the key messages emerging from this audit.

NOTES FROM THE SKILLS AND QUALITIES AUDIT

Note: Once you have done this analysis, you may like to rank the development areas, as it is always best to focus in one or two areas rather than adopting a scattergun approach.

Now that you have a better idea of your own skill level in each of the skills and qualities and have identified those you wish to develop, you can structure your development accordingly. You will also find that this audit will be useful later in this book when you read Chapters 4–8.

We will now move onto the career audit, where we encourage you to review your working life and experiences to date.

Question 1: Who am I?

Self-awareness is cited as one of the key attributes for managing a successful career in today's highly competitive and complex world.

Why is this so important? All human beings are multifaceted and incredibly challenging to understand, and this applies not only to understanding others but also to self-understanding and awareness. It is also true to say that we all evolve over time, and therefore we are ever-changing beings who have the ability to adapt and adjust to suit the various situations we find ourselves in.

In order to optimize the choices open to you in developing and managing your career options, we believe it is worthwhile taking stock and some time to explore and analyse yourself in depth. When talking to others about raising self-awareness, one of the analogies we often use is that of the onion. An onion is multilayered, much like each of you, who have many different aspects to your personality. Your behaviour is the external manifestation of your personality, but underneath this top layer there are many additional influences on the way you behave and relate to the world and the people in it. Typically, the influences that affect you include your basic personality, your values and beliefs, your strengths and weaknesses, your experiences in life, your motives, thoughts and attitudes, and much of this develops throughout your life.

Having good self-awareness enables you to have more control over the decisions you make about your life and career. Many of the decisions you make in life are based on how you interpret the situation. Typically, this is based on your current experiences, emotional responses, thoughts and understanding. Raising your self-awareness will help you to understand how your thoughts, emotions and experiences are directing your reactions and will help you to take more control over your decisions. For instance, several people in our survey commented that they had volunteered to join working parties, taken part in project teams or just taken on extra work because they felt under pressure from others to do so rather than thinking about how these activities might benefit themselves.

The only person who can answer the question 'Who Am I?' is you – no one can tell you who you are, what you want, how you should think or what you should do or believe. You must do this for yourself. What follows is a range of practical reflections and exercises that will get you started on this process of self-discovery and awareness.

Personal curriculum vitae

One technique we use when running leadership and personal development programmes and when coaching is to complete a personal curriculum vitae (CV). The idea here is to go deeper than the usual CV you may prepare for a job application. In this case, we will ask you to think through your life so far and reflect about who you are. We have presented this exercise as a table with a little space to make notes. However, some of you may find that there is insufficient space. You may need to recreate this questionnaire to enable you to make detailed notes – either in a Learning Diary or perhaps by creating a similar document on your computer.

MY PERSONAL CURRICULUM VITAE
Date of completion:
Personal Details
Current Age: Date of Birth: Currently living in: Important people in my life: Three words to describe yourself: Three words your family or friends would use to describe you: My main hobbies and interests outside work are: Achievements I am proud of: How would you describe your current work–life balance:

Professional and Work History

My current role and employer:

Time in role: Time with current employer:

Describe how you feel about your current job – likes, dislikes, challenges and frustrations:

Three words your boss would use to describe you:

Three words your colleagues would use to describe you:

Three words your team would use to describe you:

Previous role and employer:

Time in role:

Describe how you felt about this role:

Reasons for changing role:

List all previous roles, indicating time in them and what you enjoyed most about them and your reasons for moving on:

Qualifications and Education (including both formal qualifications and short training programmes)

Roles outside Work (for instance, local community work or voluntary work)

Dreams and Ambitions (describe your dream job and think about what you would ideally like from a job)

And finally – what are your realistic expectations for the next eighteen months/three years/five years?

This initial reflection and analysis may help you with some of the other exercises.

Personal values review

The way that you behave, together with your personal values, will drive many of the decisions you make in life. Your values are the gauges you use to help you assess how happy you are in relation to how you are living your life. Making a conscious effort to identify your value set will pay dividends when it comes to career planning and decision-making. For instance, understanding the values that drive you can help you to understand why:

- certain aspects of your role make you happy or unhappy
- some organizations appeal to you and some do not
- some jobs are more appealing than others
- some of the decisions you have to make at work leave you feeling unhappy

You develop your values, beliefs and attitudes throughout your life, based on the experiences you have in your family, in your work, with your friends and in the general experiences you have. Your values are those things you hold in high regard and that you use as a measure to evaluate your life. Many women tell us that compromising their values in their job causes anxiety, stress, frustration and sometimes even anger. For instance, we heard many stories of institutionalized bullying, where many of our respondents recognized what was happening yet were unable to intervene, and this left them feeling that their values were constantly being compromised.

'My values were severely challenged when I experienced an episode of bullying and even though I was a Director in the organization I had little impact on what was happening. My way of overcoming this was to leave the organization.'

'As an HR Manager I have on occasions found my values challenged when more senior people have selected a male candidate over an equally competent, and qualified woman because they feared the woman's family responsibilities would get in the way.'

'Earlier in my career I left a well-known organization when I discovered that I was being asked to communicate PR information that was skimming over some of the key issues.'

Identifying and appreciating your values and how they affect your decisions and life in general will help you to understand more about who you are and how these values inform the choices you make in life.

PERSONAL VALUES REVIEW

Stage 1: From the list below, select those values that are most important to you (use a highlighting pen) – in order to do this, you may like to ask yourself a couple of questions:
- What must be present to make me feel fulfilled and happy?
- What values must I honour and never compromise on?

The answers to these questions may help you to make your selection. Typically, most of us focus on between eight and ten values that are essential to us in living our lives. The aim is to select those values that are vital and primary to your life.

Acceptance	Empathy	Learning	Solitude
Accomplishment	Environmental	Love	Stability
Adventure	and sustainable	Loyalty	Status
Authenticity	responsibility	Making a difference	Structure
Authority	Equality	Optimism	Tact
Autonomy	Ethical values	Originality	Teamwork
Balanced	Excellence	Passion	Tolerance
Belonging	Fairness	Patience	Tradition
Broadminded	Faithfulness	Perfection	Tranquility
Caring	Family	Philanthropy	Trustworthy
Change	Forgiving	Pleasure	Uniqueness
Charitable	Freedom	Positivity	Variety
Comfort	Friendship	Power	Wealth
Compassion	Fun	Privacy	Work
Competence	Goodwill	Productivity	
Competition	Harmony	Prosperity	Add in your own
Community	Honesty	Public service	values:
Control	Honour	Punctuality	
Cooperation	Humility	Quality	
Courage	Independence	Rationality	
Courteous	Individualism	Recognition	
Creative	Influence	Reliability	
Curiosity	Innovative	Reputation	
Dedication	Integrity	Responsibility	
Devotion	Intellect	Security	
Discipline	Justice	Self-control	
Duty	Kindness	Selflessness	
Efficiency	Knowledge	Service	

Stage 2: Now rank the values you have selected in order of importance, with 1 being the most important. Indicate this ranking on the chart.

Stage 3: Now describe why each value in the ranked list is important.

1

2

3

4

5

6

7

8

9

10

Stage 4: Write down examples of times when you have lived by and demonstrated your values and the outcomes and implications of doing so.

Stage 5: Write down examples of times when you have had to compromise your values and describe the outcomes and implications of doing so.

Stage 6: Reflect back over your notes in response to this exercise and note down any insights and learning that have emerged.

Stage 7: Finally, thinking about your values and the insights you have gained, how does your current job measure up?

Personality analysis

You may have completed one or possibly more of the many personality questionnaires that are available today. Some of the most popular of these include:

- Myers Briggs Type Indicator – MBTI
- Fundamental Interpersonal Relations Orientation – Behaviour – FIRO-B
- Strength Deployment Inventory – SDI
- Occupational Personality Questionnaire – OPQ
- 16PF – Cattell's Sixteen Personality Factors
- Hogan Personality Inventory

Usually these are completed as part of a recruitment or development programme. If you have completed any of these, you should have received a comprehensive debrief and feedback on their meaning. Each and any one of these will provide you with a rich source of data and information about yourself. So, be sure to retain any data and feedback information about such questionnaires for future reference.

If, however, you have never completed a personality questionnaire, we would suggest completing Myers Briggs Type Indicator (MBTI), Strengths Deployment Inventory (SDI) or Occupational Personality Questionnaire (OPQ) all of which would be useful. Use the space below to make notes about what you have learnt about yourself from any of these questionnaires.

NOTES FROM PERSONALITY QUESTIONNAIRES
Note down the name of the questionnaire and the key insights and learning you gained.

Happiness review

Assessing your levels of overall happiness in different situations may also tell you something about who you are and what you enjoy in life. Happiness is a pretty vague notion, yet it is a fundamental human need and an idea that today's social scientists and neuroscientists are beginning to take seriously as something that contributes to our success and well-being. They believe that happy people live longer, perform better and are more resilient.

Thinking generally about your life, how would you assess your happiness level today?

So, in the context of this book, where we are looking to help you to make the most of your working life, we believe that giving some consideration to questions of happiness in relation to your job, organization and industry can contribute to understanding more about yourself and your needs.

Using the table below, assess your level of happiness in relation to each of the questions posed. For the purposes of this analysis, we are defining happiness as the levels of positivity, joy and pleasure that you get from the different areas reviewed. Having an understanding of the areas of your working life that contribute to your feelings of well-being will be beneficial. Using your responses together with some of the other exercises in this section will assist you when you come to make decisions about your future direction and plans.

MY HAPPINESS REVIEW	
Situation	**Level Of Happiness**
Current Role	Very Happy Very Unhappy _____
Previous Role	_____
Current Organization	_____
Previous Organization	_____
Current Industry	_____
Previous Industry	_____
Summarize the insights you have gained from this short survey.	

Question 2 – What have I achieved so far?

Many of us forget about achievements, skills and abilities that have been developed and demonstrated in the past. Looking back over your life to review your achievements helps you to recognize old skills that have become dormant or are now underused for some reason. It is all too easy with the passing of time to overlook things that helped you get to where you are today. Reflecting about past achievements can be energizing and rewarding, as it reminds you just how far you have come. It can also highlight skills and abilities that you may take for granted and, once prompted, can reintegrate into your repertoire to use in new contexts, often to good effect.

One of the exercises we use with groups is called 'appreciative feedback'. This exercise is a great way of learning about yourself and how other people see your achievements. The idea is that, as a group who work together on a regular basis, you get into the habit of offering each other positive feedback about what you appreciate about working with each other. Not only does this help you understand your achievements, but it will also help raise self-confidence.

In this section, we use a range of exercises to encourage readers to reflect about and analyse achievements so far.

My life timeline

A good starting point to analyse your achievements is to draw a timeline and annotate it with significant experiences and achievements as you recall them. There are many ways of doing this, but however you actually draw the line, it involves highlighting happy and unhappy memories, then using the drawing to review each of the experiences to identify learning and achievements.

Here's an example of a timeline:

Example of a Life Timeline

Happy Memories	Age	Unhappy Memories
Cast in important role in school play	7	

Passed 11+ and started new senior school	9 11	Moved to new school away from friends Felt a bit overwhelmed at first
Started at Teachers Training College	17	Got ill during the year for several weeks
Moved to London to start work Got married and moved to Hampshire Got a permanent job	18 19 21	Dropped out of college Felt lonely initially Took time to find a permanent job
Business Studies course part-time Started work as a training officer Started studying CIPD MSc in Social Research Got pregnant Daughter born and on maternity leave Moved house and got new job	23 24 26 28 29 30 31	Finding it difficult to make the move into first-level management from professional grade. Returned to work and my promotion was not to be. New job not what it promised to be so began looking for a new opportunity
Got new role as manager in Training & Development	32 33	

My Life Timeline

Happy Memories	Age	Unhappy Memories

Having created your timeline with the key events in your life, you now need to analyse it to draw out the learning and achievements.

Use the following questions as prompts:

- What have you learnt from my happy memories?
- What have you learnt from my unhappy memories?
- What did you achieve when you went through these events?
- What insights does this give you about:
  - Your skills
  - Your resilience
  - Your values
  - What's important to you
  - What you enjoy
  - What you don't enjoy
  - How well you cope in adversity

Finest moments

The idea of 'finest moments' is borrowed from the world of sport, where sportsmen and women are encouraged to record and talk about their 'personal best' performance. They reflect on what it felt like, how they prepared for it, who helped them, the learning they took away from the experience and how they can incorporate this learning into all their performances.

We have adapted this exercise and often use it on workshops or when coaching people. The aim is to get people to think about 'finest moments' or 'key events': the things they have achieved in their lives that they are proud of. By identifying these achievements, you remind yourself of times when you felt particularly fulfilled and rewarded, which helps build self-confidence. Additionally, by analysing how you did it, you will reveal skills, capabilities or talents that you may be underusing or may even have forgotten about.

We like to encourage people to think about 'finest moments' in several different areas of their lives. For instance:

- a work finest moment
- a school finest moment
- a hobby finest moment
- a family finest moment

Here are a couple of 'finest moment' examples from our research:

One of our interviewees was offered the opportunity to run a group of community-funded projects involving fifteen women leaders, all in different countries. 'We were doing some great work and I am really proud of our achievements and the fact we were helping change women's lives.' She said it was a memorable time for her, and it was only on reflection that she realized how much she'd learnt, the value of the project to building her reputation, and how important it was for her career success.

Some of the women who have attended our workshops have identified what they called 'a personal challenge' as a finest moment: for instance, running a marathon, doing the moonwalk, climbing Kilimanjaro or cycling across a desert, often while raising money for a charity. Most of these women talked about how at the beginning of these ventures they didn't realize how much they would gain from them – not least the boost to their self-belief and determination.

Use the chart below to make brief notes about your 'finest moments' and how you might use the learning drawn from this exercise in your life today and in the future. You may not be able to think of bests in all four areas, so focus on the area/s where you can easily think of one.

MY FINEST MOMENTS
In each personal best situation: • Briefly make notes about the event, situation or achievement. • Think about how it made you feel then and now – write this down. • Reflect about who helped you and how you prepared for it. • What skills or abilities did you use or develop during the process of attaining the finest moment? • What did you learn about yourself and your strengths, skills and development needs at the time and now? • How might you use this learning now and for the future?
My finest moment at ....

My finest moment at..........................

'Finest moment' is a great exercise to do with other people – by talking with a trusted other, you may find that you explore in more depth and draw more learning from the experience/s overall.

Reviewing your achievements and taking time to celebrate your successes can be surprisingly uplifting and rewarding. Not only will it remind you of previous accomplishments, but it can also help you to focus on the positive and build confidence and self-belief.

Question 3: Who supports me?

Undertaking a career audit would not be complete without examining the people in your life who have helped you get to where you are today. Recognizing who these people are, the role they have played and how they have helped you will contribute to your self-understanding and help you when it comes to planning the way ahead.

We find the following process to be a good starting point when analysing and identifying those people you believe have supported you throughout your life and career. We call this 'network mapping', and in this instance, as we are focusing on those people who have supported you throughout your career, we will call it 'My Career Support Network'.

Creating a network map is a very simple yet illuminating experience. All you need is a blank sheet of paper and a pen. Of course, in our digital age, many of you will want to use technology to create the map, so two easy ways of getting started using either a PC or a tablet are:

- On a PC, using Word, begin a Word document, select SmartArt, then use one of the relationship templates – see sample below.
- On a tablet, download the app 'SimpleMind +', which is free, though there is a sophisticated version that you can pay for. We find the free one is sufficient for our purposes.

The process is quite simple – create an image that lists all those people who have helped you in your career so far. We find that it is easiest to start with categories of people and then add their names – this makes later analysis much easier.

My career support network

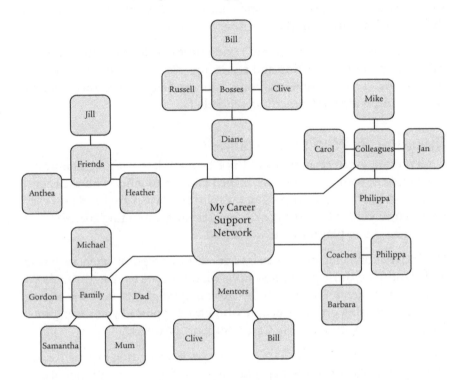

Having created the career network map, you can now begin to think about the role these people have played in your life so far and how they have supported you. There are lots of different ways of providing support, including:

- being a good listener
- offering advice
- providing developmental support
- asking searching questions
- providing feedback on behaviour and performance
- supporting your decisions and actions
- just being there for you
- sponsoring you within the organization
- acting as a coach or mentor

And, no doubt, in many other ways. For instance, one survey respondent said about support networks:

> 'I have always hesitated to ask people around me for career advice it was only when in discussion with my boss and his boss that I realized they were actually giving me advice to apply for a promotion.'

Another worthwhile question is to ask yourself which of these people have been most useful in helping you navigate your career so far, and whether they are the right people to continue to assist. If so, then plan how you will continue to work with them and how you can leverage them for even more support. If they are not the right people, you must think who else you need to add to your network and how you will do this. You might like to reflect about the balance of who supports you. For instance, have you got enough supporters at work? How would you rate your current boss – as a supporter or not? Having a supportive boss is really helpful.

Use the space below to draw your network map and then make notes about what this exercise tells you.

MY CAREER SUPPORT NETWORK MAP

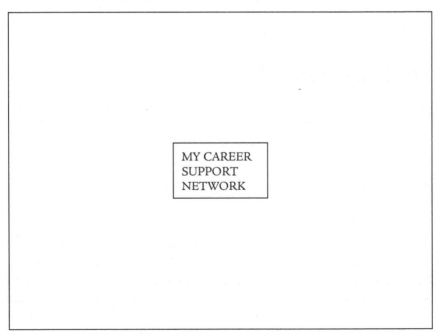

MY CAREER
SUPPORT
NETWORK

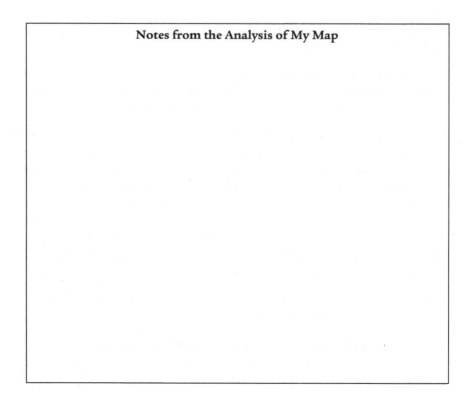

Notes from the Analysis of My Map

Feedback from others

At various points in most of our lives, we get feedback from other people. Feedback comes in many forms, both formal and informal. Formal feedback is part of organizational processes such as:

- performance reviews
- job interviews
- development programmes
- assessment centres

This feedback is often stylized and highly structured, but useful all the same. Of course, much will depend on who is giving you the feedback, but it is always worth reflecting about feedback you have received during such experiences. You might like to think about any patterns that have emerged over time.

Informal feedback is the feedback you receive on a day-to-day basis from your boss, colleagues, friends, family and others in your work and social circles. Often it goes unnoticed, and can be as simple as someone saying something like 'You are a really good listener' or 'I really like the way you handled that challenge in the meeting.' It is important to pay heed to this type of feedback as well as the more formal feedback you receive as part of your job. The informal feedback can be even more insightful than the formal kind, as it is usually given in the moment, when you have demonstrated something that has worked well. Of course, feedback can be both positive and negative, so be aware of the developmental or less positive feedback as well. For instance, if people keep saying something like "Please can you let me finish?", then it may be that the feedback you are getting is telling you that you have a problem with interrupting people. Awareness is the key here, so have your antennae constantly tuned to listen out for feedback. When you receive feedback from others, it is also worthwhile asking them to help you think through what you can do differently.

Most people do not ask for feedback. We find that actually asking others for feedback is incredibly useful, especially if you frame the feedback around a specific issue or behaviour: for instance, asking a trusted colleague to comment on your listening skills at the end of a meeting that you chaired. One way of building your confidence and self-awareness is to get used to asking others for specific feedback on a regular basis. You might also wish to take opportunities to offer feedback to others when they perform well.

There are several benefits in making this part of your work ethic: you

- begin to create a feedback culture in your work environment
- build good-quality trusting relationships
- develop confidence and self-efficacy
- develop new skills
- increase your self-awareness
- demonstrate emotional acuity

The issue with feedback is that it is a valuable indicator of your behaviour and what works and what doesn't work for others. Sometimes we gain insights from the views of others about things we ourselves are not aware of.

Question 4: What am I looking for in my work?

So, what are you looking for from your work? When we ask people this question, we are often surprised at how few people are able to clearly articulate what they seek. However, it is important to add here that any answers you do give to this question should be grounded in what's possible.

The answers we often hear are:

- I'd like to work with people
- I want to be a manager
- I want to work for a well-known organization
- I want to help others
- I want to do something that I am good at
- I want to work somewhere with good promotion prospects
- I want to do a job that satisfies me
- I want something with travel opportunities
- I want to work in ... (marketing, PR, travel, etc.)

It is far more effective if you are like Carina, an IT specialist, who, when asked during a career coaching session, was able to express the following as her job requirements:

'I enjoy being part of a team who are creating something new in the technology field. I think my future lies in a small organization or a start-up where I will have the opportunity to use my skills and not be hampered by hierarchy and bureaucracy. Location is not an issue for me in fact I am happy to move to find the right job. Salary and package wise I want to feel that I am being rewarded appropriately for what I am doing but for the right job this would not be a deal breaker. The deal breaker for me would be if the company lacked moral integrity.'

It is important to say that this information emerged in our third meeting, after we had spent some time working through her career so far and encouraging her to do some of the reflections that we have suggested in this chapter. As she was able to express her requirements so clearly, we were then able to move forward to work on a practical action plan for the future.

For those of you who are not as clear as Carina about your ideals, here are a few exercises that may help you to develop greater clarity. We will start with a Job Environment Review in which we will ask you to indicate your preferences in a list of different scenarios. Look at the list of situations below and indicate with a tick the work scenarios that appeal to you.

Job environment review

JOB ENVIRONMENT REVIEW Indicate with a tick ✓ those environments that appeal to you.					
Public sector		Private sector		Voluntary sector	
Multinational company		Local organization		National company	
Start-up		Well-established sector		Well-known brand	
				Director level	
Part of a team		Team leader		Manager level	
Specialist		Generalist		People oriented	
Security		Independence		Problem-solving orientation	
Autonomy		Structure		Being influential	
Flexible hours		Part-time		Full-time	
Learning environment		Promotion opportunities		Travel opportunities	
Fits with family responsibility		Completely free agent		Limited responsibility	
Creative orientation					
Add in your own ideas:					

Looking at this review, make notes about those environments that seem to resonate for you.

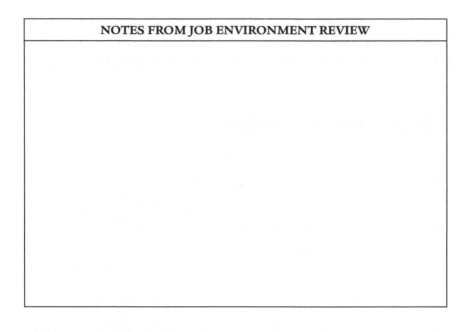

NOTES FROM JOB ENVIRONMENT REVIEW

Edgar Schein's career anchors

Another area you may like to consider was developed by Edgar Schein and is called 'career anchors'. A career anchor is defined as 'your unique combination of perceived career competence, motives and values' and is identified by completing a forty-item questionnaire that will help you to think about what you want out of a career. The questionnaire is based on eight career anchors that Schein has identified. Each of these anchors suggests a vital element of your job for career satisfaction:

- Technical/Functional – using a technical or functional skill
- General Management – being responsible and accountable for results
- Autonomy/Independence – being responsible for what you do and how you do it
- Security/Stability – working in a secure and stable environment
- Entrepreneurial Creativity – creating your own organization or business
- Service/Dedication to a Cause – achieving something of value
- Pure Challenge – having the opportunity to compete and win some-times against the odds
- Lifestyle – flexibility to ensure life/work balance

Understanding your primary career anchor can help you to understand your preferences for certain aspects of your job and will help you manage your career planning and decision-making. You can find the question-naire at careeranchorsonline.com, where it can be purchased. Once it is completed, you will receive a personalized report that explains your career anchor as well as a detailed description of the other seven categories.

'What if question'

This exercise is based on an idea used in Solution-Focused Coaching, where people are asked to suspend judgement and do some free-fall thinking about the issue being discussed at the coaching session. We want you to apply this idea to your thoughts about your future career. So think about everything you have learnt about yourself and your job ambitions so far. Now free-fall and think about it as if there were no restrictions or limitations on what you could do. Write a short description (in the box below) about what your ideal job would be. Try to be as descriptive and specific as possible.

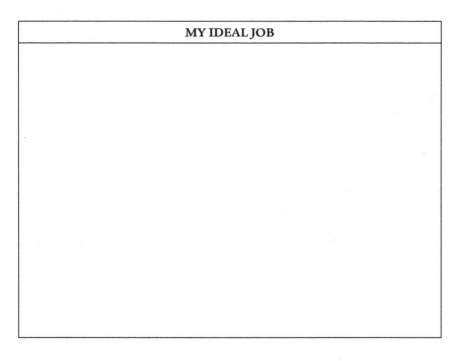

MY IDEAL JOB

Ideals are not always achievable, so review and consider what the key elements are from your description above, what's possible for you and how you might pursue these ideals. For instance, having done this exercise, many women tell us that they realize one thing that is holding them back is lack of a formal qualification or more technical expertise, and in doing this they realize that one way of pursuing their ideal is to get qualified or get some training. As a few of our respondents said,

> 'I eventually realized that not having a degree was holding me back. So, I made a business case and persuaded my employer to fund vocational training.'

> 'Having left school at 16 I was a bit of an idiot until I was in my late 20s. If I'd put as much energy into my career as I did into my social life I would have been a world-beater. I turned it around by going to university at 30 and getting a 2:1.'

> 'After 5 years as a hairdresser I realized I was bored and had lost my motivation until I won a place on a Diploma course to give me specialist skill in hair colouring. This was a prestigious course in my field and involved a lot of hard work, study and practical work, and not everyone stayed the course. Adding this extra string to my bow was the motivation I needed – all the hard work was worthwhile.'

Question 5: How will I achieve my dreams?

Achieving your dreams can, on occasion, be due to circumstance and luck, but in our view, having a strategy, ideas and plans leads to greater success and enables you to adapt and flex throughout your journey.

A popular exercise to help you organize your thoughts and review your strengths, weaknesses, opportunities and threats is called a Strengths, Weaknesses, Opportunities & Threats (SWOT) analysis. This is an adaptation of a well-used strategic management tool. It is very easy to apply and can be helpful in reviewing your current skill set, areas for development, and those aspects of your life that you consider to be opportunities and threats.

Use the chart below to note down your answers to all or some of the following questions. Use the questions that help you the most in each of the four areas:

- Strengths
    - What am I good at?
    - What personal characteristics give me an advantage over others?
    - Compared with others, what do I do better?
    - How would my bosses describe my strengths?
    - What would my team/colleagues describe as my strengths?
    - What values and attitudes contribute towards my skill set?
    - What personality traits contribute to my strengths?

- Weaknesses
    - What am I not so good at and avoid doing?
    - What personal characteristics do I believe to be a disadvantage?
    - How would others describe my weaknesses – bosses, colleagues, team, etc....?
    - What skills am I not so confident using?

- Opportunities
    - How well networked are you with people to support and advise you?
    - What is happening now in your organization/profession/industry that could provide an opportunity for you?
    - Are there situations in your life/work that you could exploit for greater success?
    - Are you leveraging your strengths to best advantage?

- Threats
    - How are you working to alleviate your weaknesses, to capitalize on these skills/abilities and turn them into opportunities?
    - Are there situations in your life/work that could prove to be hazards to your success?
    - What impediments exist in your life/work at the moment? Think about technology, networks, changing circumstances, etc....

PERSONAL SWOT ANALYSIS

STRENGTHS	WEAKNESSES
OPPORTUNITIES	THREATS

A personal SWOT analysis is best done when you need to organize information to help you review an aspect of your life. It can assist in your decision-making about career, work and life issues by helping you to understand more about yourself, enabling you to capitalize on your strengths and opportunities when making important decisions in your life.

Career audit reflections

We have introduced you to many self-analysis ideas in this chapter. It is now important to summarize your key thoughts so far.

SUMMARY SO FAR

In writing this summary, you may find some of the following questions useful.

What have you found out about yourself that is new?

What have you found out about yourself that is important for your career/job now and in the future?

How satisfied are you in your current job?

Have you identified any pressure or stress areas that you need to deal with?

What changes do you anticipate making in the short term/long term?

Have you identified any development needs – for example, skills to develop, job or project secondment opportunities, formal training, etc....?

And finally:

The purpose of this book is to help you get the most from your job/career/ profession and to feel fulfilled and satisfied in whatever you are doing or choose to do in the future. We have purposely not focused this book on 'getting to the top' because we believe that for many, the goal is to have a satisfying and rewarding job and career, not necessarily to get to the top, break the glass ceiling or be a leader. As many of you tell us, 'I just want a satisfying and rewarding job, a fair workplace and a feeling that I am not being disadvantaged simply because of my gender.' Our motivation to write this book came from the need to provide a structured approach for career reflection and planning: something that too few of you make time to do in your busy lives.

Remember, age is no barrier to change, nor does it matter what stage of career you are at. For instance, we know people who have changed direction in their 30s, 40s and 50s – it's always possible. For instance, Carolyn McCall moved from the media newspaper business to be chief executive at EasyJet Airline, one woman in our survey decided in her mid-30s to retrain from being a nurse to becoming a paediatrician, and another left a well-paid job in the City to set up a vineyard.

Later in this book, we offer ideas on how you can develop yourself in a range of skills and qualities that you need in your career. Towards the end, we also talk about how you can make it all happen. Remember, it is valuable to have a story to tell at any stage in your life about the way you see your career unfolding, your ambitions and your ideas for your career journey. The purpose of doing a career audit and all the other exercises in this book is to help you be more focused, more confident, able to talk about your achievements, what you want to do next and in the future.

Chapter 2

Women's experiences: What they say

We asked women in an online survey during the summer of 2015 to tell us about their career experiences and received over 1,400 responses. We also interviewed a number of women to delve deeper into their life, work and career experiences. As you might expect we heard many, many personal success stories, many examples about what has helped them to be successful and what has blocked their career. The range and breadth of their experiences and what they say is a valuable insight into the career journeys of working women today.

The women represent a wide variety of age ranges, occupations, sectors, countries, nationalities and levels: doctors, teachers, lawyers, pilots, buyers, statisticians, accountants, solicitors, product managers, politicians, civil servants, academics, engineers, cabin crew, learning and development and HR professionals, journalists, administrators, and those working in hi-tech, advertising, marketing, PR and across a variety of sectors including voluntary, pharma, financial services, tobacco, service sector, energy, arts, theatre and museums, the National Health Service, local and national government and retail, and automotive. We may not have heard about every job, management level or sector, but we have heard from a wide cross-sector of working women.

While most of the women were based in the UK, we also heard from many who lived and worked in global and international roles, as well as women from Switzerland, Turkey, Scandinavia, Greece, Denmark, Italy, Germany, North America, France, Spain, the Middle East, Australia, Malaysia, Japan and China. Some are just at the start of their career, many others are mid-way or at the most senior levels, and some are entrepreneurs or have chosen freelance work. There are those who are taking time out for family reasons and others who have stories to tell about being a working mother. Employers include public, private and voluntary sectors, ranging from micro to mid-size firms, right up to multinational giants.

In our survey, one of the questions asked women to tell us about the barriers they have faced in their working life. Some women could honestly say that they had encountered no barriers during their career at all. It is great to hear this news, and this was equally likely to be said by women of any age or career stage. Others felt that the only barriers they found were those created by themselves – such as lack of confidence or what is known as the 'imposter syndrome', in which someone feels they should not have the success or senior job that they have won. For example, many women spoke about their lack of confidence, including many successful senior women, for instance, Jayne-Anne Gadhia, who is the recently appointed chief executive of Virgin Money. You can read more about confidence in Chapter 5.

As one survey respondent told us,

'I have been my own worst barrier. ... Almost on autopilot, and it is only in recent years that a good mentor has helped me realise that I have actually crafted a fairly decent career all things considered.'

It is worth saying here that it does sometimes take a while to recognize that any one of us may unintentionally put up our own barriers: a person who decides not to apply for a new job or promotion may be worried that they could fail, or that their new colleagues may not like them. There is also evidence of ageism, and this may be unintentional on the part of employers, as shown in the following quote:

'I now feel that the main barrier to my career at the moment is age. Over the past few years the recruitment strategy is to recruit graduates and provide in-house training. This means the opportunities for anyone like me who is already HR qualified and over 40 are limited. The impact of this on me has been that I am less likely to apply for jobs as I know these will be reserved for graduates.'

Some women work in male-dominated sectors such as engineering and manufacturing, and many mention the fact that while there may be women at more junior levels, there are few women decision-makers. This means that there is a lack of role models – something that we know makes a difference in terms of whether women believe that they, too, might reach senior levels in a company.

It might be assumed that 'being a woman in a man's world' was something more likely to be said about careers of the past, and yet it seems to remain as a modern theme as well, often in new industries such as robotics and video game design. Perhaps, though, it is not as prevalent as it once was, and of course, there are many areas – such as marketing, advertising and journalism – that have seen seismic change and where women can definitely be said to hold their own. But it is not true everywhere, and in certain sectors, or at more senior levels, inequality remains a problem.

'I'm dealing with men who don't think engineering is a place for women.'

'I'm the only woman in this company working as an engineering specialist and this makes me feel very isolated.'

Many of the experiences women described to us offer some practical learning and highlight what we have called multipliers and derailers.

- Career multipliers are events and opportunities that are good for your career.
- Career derailers are events and issues that are barriers, blocks or things that delay your career.

Later in this chapter, we focus on the practical aspects of 'challenges and solutions' that women have found. If you are experiencing your own career challenge at the moment, please don't be disappointed if you do not find it mentioned in this book, but be reassured that there will be a way around the problem. You may need someone to advise you, or try a few different approaches and keep trying. Be creative, be patient and above all, be determined. One of the qualities we admired in many of the women interviewed for this book is their determination, flexibility and stick-ability, as illustrated below:

'I changed career direction 5 times – working in Greece (and learning to speak the language), running projects across different EU member countries. Then I set up my own successful training company that I ran for a number of years before moving back to the UK and taking a PhD qualification. Most recently I now work in executive search.'

'I started my career in the NHS as a Dietician and then pursued 3 different career paths which involved retraining and further degree qualifications. Throughout this time there was constant restructuring and reorganization which meant my role was often "at risk" and in fact I was made redundant 7 times over the years. Eventually I did indeed succeed in breaking through the glass ceiling of NHS Senior Management and went on to become CEO of a primary care group.'

Both these stories illustrate multitalent and flexibility, as well as determination that has brought the women through varied and sometimes difficult career journeys.

Career multipliers

The term 'career multipliers' is all about opportunities that propel your career forward, and those things that make a big difference to your career potential, which can affect your expertise, experience or level of confidence: for instance, a chance to gain management experience early on in your career, to take an international assignment, to attend a management development programme or to job shadow a senior manager, to mention just a few. Role models and a supportive boss can also help you a great deal, especially early on in your career. If your first boss is supportive (and also a good manager), then it's a bit like what happens in a relay race: you are off to a good start. But, if they are poor, indifferent or downright bad, then this invariably will impact on you. There's nothing quite like that feeling of a great job well done and being congratulated. For instance, one woman told us that when she won a large contract, her boss was so delighted that he offered to pay the expenses for her weekend away, which was already booked. He also made a big fuss in the company, with cakes and celebrations, so that everyone knew her role in winning this piece of important work.

Another example is about one of the women we interviewed for this book, who is now a freelance director of photography, cinematographer, lighting cameraperson and camera operator. Earlier in her career, she was encouraged to apply for a scheme to work alongside an important director of photography as he made the film *The Golden Compass*. It doesn't get much better than that in terms of learning your skills from someone who is at the top of the tree, though it nearly didn't happen:

'I was encouraged to apply for the technical change scheme by another organization simply because if no-one applied then the network would lose this funding. I enjoyed what I was doing as a Focus Puller (Camera Assistant) and at that stage did not feel that motivated to change. I really did not expect the application would go any further but then heard I'd been selected for an interview and then I was offered the opportunity! But I wasn't sure what to do at this point. I'd just split up with my fiancé a few days before and because it was unexpected I had nowhere else to go but my parents' house. The Director asked me what was going on in my life right now and I had to be honest; I told him about the split and that I didn't know what I was going to do or where I was going to live. However, he saw things differently to me. Instead of being a time of confusion for me he thought it was great timing; that I should stay with my parents and spend the year being mentored by him and focussing on my career development.'

A number of survey respondents mention the opportunity to join a company-wide project team. Often such teams are organized in a hurry with specific, rather challenging goals, but they are great places to get noticed by other more senior people, to develop new relationships and, of course, improve your knowledge of other business areas.

Mentoring is another great career multiplier for supporting your development and career potential. However, there's often a certain unwarranted mystique about how it happens, which means that women don't find mentors! As one of our interviewees commented,

'I've always been mentored by men and I don't think it matters if it is a man or woman who helps you. Some people think it should be a woman but I don't agree with this view.'

We'd say the same, and indeed, some of the mentors in both our careers have been men.

'I realise now that early in my career I had some great mentors and people who supported me.'

Karen Lord, who is the first woman to run the John Lewis Oxford Street branch, recently gave some practical advice about this – she said, 'Don't wait for your mentor to come to you.' Instead, said Karen, 'Go out and find your mentors. Make sure you find the right person and be specific about what you want to develop – and why.' Karen was speaking at a Red Women event – more information about this can be found at www.redonline.co.uk.

Career multipliers can arrive in many different shapes and forms – and often women say that at the time they don't realize quite how important these things are. So you need to recognize them and to seek out different options that can help your career develop. For example:

- If you are a teacher or consultant, organizing a workshop at the next regional event in your area. Not only will you meet people as a result; it also says something about you and your abilities that will set you apart from others. So when you go for a new job, your CV will stand out from the others.
- Moving to a new job and finding a boss who believes in you, recognizes your abilities and offers support to help you develop your career. 'I always had great support from my bosses who helped me to move in my career. They have stayed around as well as mentors throughout the following years.'
- Taking an MBA or a professional qualification – as one woman explained, 'This meant studying in the evenings and on weekends to ensure I finished with a good mark and enabled me to enhance my career opportunities.' Another respondent studied hard for a PhD, recognizing that this not only gave her more knowledge but would enhance her employability.

The top career multipliers most frequently mentioned during our research include:

- Having **a good boss** who offers support and challenge: it is notable how much difference there is in 'support and challenge'. You can learn quite a lot when you receive support from colleagues or your boss, but someone, more experienced, who offers support **and** challenge means that you develop skills you didn't know you had!
- Building a good **network** of people who show faith in you and guide and push you to move from your comfort zone. A network should both be within your organization and include external relationships as well.
- **Determination and tenacity**: working hard, persistence, giving your all to the job and delivering over and above your goals and objectives.
- Good **communication skills**: asking the right questions: speaking up for yourself and in presentations.
- **Energy and enthusiasm**: we don't mean enjoying your job or working for a great company – though that's always important. We're talking about your contribution; it's about the 'Lean in' principles that Sheryl Sandberg describes in her book. If you are always keen, enthusiastic

and full of energy, then you are an asset and a great member of any team. People want to have you around them, as you help build everybody's energy levels. You need to make a positive difference wherever you are: at a meeting, in a team or in your company. Don't ever be a 'sleeping partner'; try instead to be positive and to make a difference, thus contributing to your credibility and reputation.

- **Career planning**: there is no substitute for career planning. It makes all the difference in helping you discover what you like and what you are good at, and understanding potential barriers that may get in your way.
- **Having a mentor!** In addition to a mentor, a sponsor and a coach are also useful supporters to help you build your career.

Now let's change direction and consider what it is that can sabotage your career or stop it dead in the water.

Career derailers

As you might expect, derailers are the issues that push you off your career journey, delay you or block your ambition. Losing a job would be one example, or the difficulties in finding a new one. One survey respondent said,

'I applied for over 200 jobs before I heard back from Tesco ... thank goodness they did reply and I did get the job.'

Another example is losing the passion you once held for your job when you feel 'stuck' or in a dead end. This can be a very difficult place to be for any length of time and will challenge your levels of motivation. You should also pay careful attention to making sure you don't suffer from depression if such a situation goes on for any length of time.

There are always events that can derail your career, such as a bout of ill-health, redundancy, falling victim to office politics or taking on a role that has limited opportunities for development and progression. Another example is too much job-hopping – you might think that moving jobs every twelve to eighteen months is a good way of gaining more variety and experience, but it's a paradox. If you think about how you might feel as a prospective employer, it looks as if you get bored quickly and may therefore be a risky person to hire, so you need to be aware of such issues.

One of the most likely derailer comments made by women in our survey was about the problems of being a working mother, and for some the scary time of taking a few years off when the family are young. It may not be surprising to know that this often knocks women's confidence, and while even a few months out of the working cycle is difficult, a longer time away is harder still. One young working mother who came back after a nine-month break following the birth of her second daughter said,

> 'There had been so much change that I hardly recognised the place. My job was still there, yes ... But it was almost like starting at a new company.'

And it's probably true to say that most employers, and all of us as colleagues, don't recognize how hard it might be or do enough to help.

A wide range of derailers were mentioned. The most frequent derailers mentioned by our interviewees and survey respondents are:

- **Career sacrifice to prioritize children and other family members**. By far the most frequently mentioned derailer or barrier to career success. 'Having a child meant that I am sacrificing a career for flexibility and convenience to ensure I can prioritise my child.' 'Having children also slowed my progression, mainly because I wanted it all, to be a brilliant and attentive mother as well as a driven career woman. Balancing these two and dealing with the constant guilt of feeling like you should be somewhere else meant that things had to be put on hold for a while.'

  In the same context, many also mentioned lack of support from family, partner and/or husband. For some women, it was a conscious choice to invest time and commitment to their children. Other women also mentioned being the trailing/following spouse when their partner moved to new locations to take advantage of new roles: 'Being married to a husband who likes to move around.'

- **Lack of good childcare** and lack of flexible working options for working mothers. There is so much more that employers could do – each and every town could develop shared systems to help working parents, and organizations could have on-site nurseries. 'Childcare was an obstacle, I waited until the youngest child started school before retraining.' A few companies are leading the way in this respect, such as the Toyota car plant at Burnaston, Derbyshire. One woman, who is an engineering section manager at the plant, used the on-site crèche (with options for shift workers), and this meant she was able to return to work after her son was born.

- Having an **unsupportive or bad boss**. This may not simply be about someone whom you don't get on with; it can be about someone who is not particularly skilled as a manager. 'Having a manager who didn't give me credit or room to grow.' Many women mentioned bosses (including women!) who felt threatened by talented women, who didn't give credit for good work, bullied or belittled them, and were actively hostile towards working mothers. 'My most important barrier was a boss who felt threatened by ambitious talented women.'

- The difficulties of working in an **all-male team** or a male-dominated environment with a strong '**old boys' network**' that influenced working practices, promotion and the working environment. Sexism and gender bias in certain environments: for example, IT, financial services and higher education were mentioned as places where 'women apparently have to prove themselves much more than their male peers.' 'There is an old boys' network where they promote each other.'

- Being **a square peg in a round hole** – feeling that you either don't like your job, it is not the ideal job you dreamt about, or it's not the job you were promised when recruited. This can lead to lack of confidence and self-belief.

- **Stereotypes about working mothers** – we heard stories from women in many different sectors and organizations about the assumptions often made about working mothers. For instance, one popular myth is that working mothers are not serious about their career or taking on major responsibility: 'In our company I notice that pregnancy, maternity and just generally being a woman is perceived by others to be prioritising their children rather than their job – this can definitely be a barrier to career progression here.' Others relate to business travel, promotion, moving locations or taking on an international assignment.

- **Ageism** – being too young or too old. It seems that many assumptions are made about age and some jobs – 'initially my age was a barrier – it was felt that I was too young to move into an administrator role when I was in my early 20s, as existing administrators were all around 40.' There are often perceptions about age and promotion – 'senior leaders in my team feel that one has to be a certain age to be promoted.' At the other end of the scale, it seems that as women get older they are also disadvantaged – 'I have also started to experience ageism, but only when I hit 50.'

- **Having to compromise your values** – when a job conflicts with your personal values: 'I left a senior role as I did not like the way we were asked to treat our students.' Working in an environment where your values are regularly challenged, either by the organizational strategy and processes or by things you have to do as part of your role, can lead to disenchantment, which in turn can lead to derailment.
- **Staying too long** in one organization, which led to standing still or not winning promotion, as one woman commented: 'I worked for more than 11 years at my government department and did not advance. I had to change work completely and move to a local government role and I soon won promotion there. But if I had not left the first job then I would still be a desk officer there.'
- **Blatant discrimination** – we were surprised to hear a number of stories about discrimination. It seems rather an old-fashioned concept for the twenty-first century, and we might have hoped that it had all disappeared by now. Some examples included: 'I have been openly told that taking maternity leave is taking the mick.' 'In my early career I was not recruited to a trainee management programme as they thought I was likely to get pregnant and take maternity leave.' 'When I was looking for my first GP appointment I was asked (by a woman) at the interview whether I intended to start a family!' '"My dear girl" is still a relatively common way for a male colleague to undermine a woman's authority.'

Some quotes below illustrate a few other different, often industry-specific, stories and themes that we heard about:

'The main barrier for me as a junior doctor was having to work 80-120 hours a week in the formative years of my career. This led to much sleep deprivation and I felt disillusioned with medicine as a career.'

'I really wanted a job in HR when I left university but everywhere I applied to only wanted people with experience of HR – but I couldn't get this experience!'

'Young female colleagues underestimate the male system (in Germany), they think that education and enough effort will be sufficient to succeed.'

A number of women mentioned subtle issues that block or derail them, such as:

'A lack of awareness of some bridges you need to cross'

(specifically, the importance of being visible to other more senior people in your organization).

'I was unaware that I wasn't very visible in my previous role. If all was going well – and it mostly was – I wasn't summoned to explain myself and so gradually I realised that more senior managers didn't know me or the work I was doing ... I then worked on my presentation skills significantly and volunteered myself to speak at leadership forums.'

This chapter is intended to set out the issues, rather than to discuss coping strategies or specific solutions for each and every issue. However, if you currently feel you are facing a derailing issue in your career, then the following practical advice may help you.

Dealing with derailers – four key steps

Step 1: Identify the issue that is blocking you and set out the 'facts' objectively.

Step 2: Think about the impact this situation has on you – how does it make you feel? And why?

Step 3: Share this information with someone else. The worst thing you can do in this situation is to bottle it all up inside, as this often means you can suffer physical symptoms such as headaches, irritability or prolonged bouts of insomnia. Be aware that these types of symptoms are the body's way of coping with a bad situation and are an early 'pay attention warning sign'. If you don't pay attention, then you may become very ill indeed. The pressure can also make you 'explode', just as a fizzy drink will explode under severe pressure!

We would not advise you to leave a job until you have another one – this is why Step 4 below is so important. We would also advise you to leave on good terms. You might be tempted to tell everyone how miserable you have been, but do resist this temptation. You just don't know when or if you might need to be in touch again.

Step 4: Think about:

- coping strategies – these are very important if you can't change things immediately
- setting out a plan of action to change what's happening

The purpose of this chapter is to help you understand the power of career multipliers – and encourage you to go out and find these – and to appreciate how much derailers can slow you down.

Think about your own experiences:

	Examples from your career	Personal learning from this
Career multipliers		
Career derailers		

Headlines from this chapter

It is clear that there are few set rules about modern careers and women's experiences. It is, however, true that there is less career advice and support available these days. Some employers provide good structures, mentoring, training and coaching, but many do not. This, therefore, makes it far more important for individuals to take responsibility for their own career development.

Have a career strategy! It's really important to build your career, develop your skills and widen your experience. Don't just keep your head down and do your job, but look at what's happening around you and take an interest in other parts of the company where you are working. Be aware of any derailers that happen to you and take action to resolve such problems. Be aware of the power of multipliers and make sure you look for these. Don't just wait to be invited.

A career journey is sometimes easy and sometimes difficult. There are certain themes we have explored in this chapter that may help you understand whether you are 'on track' or 'off track' in terms of where you would like to be in the next four to five years. A number of the women we spoke to for this book who are coming towards the end of their careers wish that they had been more ambitious, looked for more adventurous careers, and had more feedback and career advice early on in their career. There is a certain Catch-22 in some career situations: for example, you are unlikely to become a chief executive in a public limited company if you have not had an operational, financial or international role. Similarly, while there may be some gender issues about saying you are ambitious (there are some national ones as well), if you don't say what you want then it's hardly surprising if people around you don't think you are career minded.

Another gender issue that we should mention is that women are sometimes too cooperative at work compared with their male colleagues, who are more selective – and that women will take on any task they are asked to, simply because they are asked! So, check and make sure this does not adversely affect your career.

It's also an unfortunate fact of modern-day working life that a number of proxy (and sometimes highly irrelevant) facts are used to determine whether someone is serious about their career. Long hours at the office are one; another is frequent travel or location moves.

It is important that you are outspoken in asking for career opportunities. We know that women are sometimes less likely to expect as much as men. Of course, many good employers recognize that this does happen, but you have to drive your own career forward. So, think about these points, together with the following:

- **Strategize and plan your career** – wherever you are now in your career, review where you are, and if you want to change, then develop a strategy for the future. Even large organizations these days are delayered, with fewer opportunities for promotion and moving around.
- **Take opportunities**, ask for opportunities and above all, look for opportunities. Not every promotion is advertised across a company, and many projects start, stop and restart informally as and when they suit different business needs.
- **Invest in relationships** and understand the power of networking – it is often through networks and other people that doors open to different opportunities.
- **Invest in and build your skills**. Ask your company for training and development, search out career advice either inside or outside the company. Professional associations, conferences and women's networks will usually provide you with access to events and introduce you to resources you can use.
- **Value feedback and understand the impression you are creating** – if you know how others see you, this can help you with your image and your promotability. In many organizations, someone is likely to be admired for bringing in new, innovative ideas or for managing change well, so think about what people would say about you. What is your image in the company? Do people see you as smart, energetic and a go-getter or merely a good worker who waits to be told what to do? Think about the impression other people in your company have of you, and consider how you manage your reputation and build your credibility.
- **Work smarter, not simply harder**. Look carefully, and frequently, at how you can be more effective and how your team can work better together. Don't just accept a task and work away at it until it is finished. Consider the best way to do the job and the most effective use of the resources you have available to you.

- **Learn how to be resilient** and how best to deal with setbacks. This is really important, and some companies recognize that how a person deals with adversity is an important way of selecting candidates for more senior roles.
- **Be aware of the gender gap** and be sure that there is a level playing field in the ways that you are treated compared with your male colleagues. They may get offered more career multipliers than you do!
- **Understand and recognize the 'imposter syndrome'** – described at the start of this chapter. If this is something you suffer from, identify it and develop a coping strategy.

Finally,

Some of the career dilemmas and the solutions we heard about from our interviewees and survey respondents include:

'I am certain that I have not been considered for promotion on certain opportunities because of being female, I do have three children but I think it was the woman rather than the mother that was being denied opportunities. I don't think I did overcome the barriers, I have progressed in spite of them by demonstrating competence and professionalism and never used my childcare responsibilities as an excuse for not doing anything which often resulted in hugely complicated domestic disruption and occasionally real personal sadness and distress.'

'There was a barrier until 2009 non-lawyers were not able to become Partners in Law Firms due to the rules of the Law Society.
When this changed I became one of the first non-lawyers appointed.'

'My managers (both women) were totally unsympathetic and in fact were part of the problem of being able to balance new work demands with being a mother. In the end I overcame this by leaving the company taking my career in a different direction. With hindsight, the experience did me a great favour but it was very difficult at the time.'

You may also find it useful to use the blank form that follows to describe how you have resolved any of your own career dilemmas.

And remember, there is no career problem that you cannot resolve! All of them have solutions.

Your Career Dilemma	Solution

Chapter 3

Where are you in your career?

Whether you are just starting out on your working life or in mid-flight with maybe a few doubts about what you should do next, then we think this chapter will help you. We will introduce you to a framework to help you think about where you are in your career, and we will encourage you to reflect about the route you have followed and the various choices you have made and transition points you have experienced. In Chapter 1, we offered you a more detailed review – a career audit – but in this chapter we would like to start you thinking more broadly on a few different topics:

- About your life (section 1).
- Consider where you are in your career/life (section 2).
- Think about a few of the choices you have faced (or may in future face) in your career (section 3).
- Stories about career challenges women have faced and how they have overcome these issues (section 4).

Each section is designed to be pretty much self-contained, so feel free to dip in anywhere you like. If you prefer, however, you can look at each section in turn. Careers in this day and age are very different from how they were, say, ten or fifteen years ago. Some large employers still have an annual graduate recruitment process, hi-fliers programmes (for those identified as having the potential for more senior roles) and clear career pathways. However, many do not, and often, even in large companies, there may not be clear career routes to show you how to progress within functions, such as marketing, or across the different business areas. But even if you do work for an employer with crystal-clear career advice and pathways, our advice would still be the same – do not take a passive role in all of this; you need to take responsibility for your own career journey and development.

So let's begin by saying something about what sometimes holds women back in their careers – and this is a really important point – because sometimes it is you who put the brakes on your career ambitions and seeking the right job. Just think about the following comments:

'I know I should move on and find another job but it feels comfortable here – I know everyone.'

'I'm a key member of the team: I can't possibly move.'

'My boss relies on me so I won't move until they do.'

'I'm not sure I have the right experience for the job I've just heard about.'

'I'm stuck in a job I hate but I don't know what to move to so I'll probably just end up staying here.'

Does any of this sound familiar? Sometimes it will be family and personal issues that constrain you, as happened for someone who now holds a senior appointment in the public sector:

I was looking for an employer where I could combine my family role and my work interests as I finished my PhD at Manchester with modest hopes, thinking that, if only I can find a part-time teaching role in further education then I'll be happy. However, I was lucky and in my first appointment at a university I found a place where I could develop my skills and research interests, something that was important to me.

Other times it can be lack of confidence that means it's more comfortable to stay where you are, which seems to be a particular issue for women. You might like to read the research by two American journalists, Kay and Shipman, about how this lack of confidence is stopping women from climbing the business career ladder or achieving their potential.

So it's important to know that you can learn confidence – in exactly the same way that you can learn finance, leadership, marketing, art or quantum physics. One of the women we interviewed for this book took up ballet classes when she was young because she was shy and wanted to change that. Other simple techniques we've heard about include:

- Going out of your way to do more presentations – the more you do, the better you will get. You may not ever be totally comfortable with them, but you can, and you should, do them, as the opposite approach – of avoiding – makes it still harder to do them at any future date.
- Volunteering for a role that means writing business proposals – a new skill. Not only do you learn more about the company, but it usually means you are working with different colleagues and clients.

- Gaining people skills early on, for instance, in a part-time job while at university – working in any customer-facing role is also great for learning influencing skills! If you can manage to cope with a difficult customer, this is the type of experience that will help you in any difficult workplace situation.

If someone strides out and walks in a more bullish way, they seem to others to be confident; they may be confident, or not. And someone who is always prepared to speak out at a business meeting seems confident, but we have no idea of how they feel inside. Take a look at Amy Cuddy's TED Talk at www.ted.com. With over twenty-six million views, it's the second most popular TED Talk, which seems to suggest that there are many people who may struggle with confidence levels. A number of women who responded to our survey highlighted the fact that taking time away from work to raise children was a key moment when their confidence dipped (or slipped completely).

So, you can change your own approach and learn confidence. It can also come from others around you, and support from colleagues, and a boss who praises you in team meetings and tells everyone how great you are, will definitely help boost your confidence. But if you should be unfortunate enough to work in what we would call a 'thanks-free' zone, an environment where you hear no praise but instead are regularly called to account for what's wrong, this will sap your confidence and your energy levels. You might like to reflect on the following statements:

Statement	Yes	No	Notes
My working environment is one that builds my levels of self-confidence			
I create a working environment for others that builds levels of self-confidence			
I work in a team where people are generous with praise			
I regularly receive development and training opportunities			

Every company, regardless of size and sector, should offer regular development and training opportunities. Attending such events will help you understand your own skills, strengths and development areas. Remember this when you are considering moving to a new employer – a company that does not offer any is unlikely to see people development as important. This may make you think twice before joining such an organization.

Reflection. Spend a while thinking about your level of self-confidence and the implications of this for your career.

The next section looks at where you are in your life.

Section 1: About your life

Thinking about how you spend your time currently is a good idea, and we've also set out below a question about your 'ideal' situation, as this is often different from the current situation.

You may also like to pause and reflect upon where most of your energy goes. Do you behave differently in different places? Someone was asked recently about what it was like to live with the amazing, energizing boss whom everyone in the office admired and enjoyed working with. Surely, they assumed, it must be a similar fantastic environment when she was with her family and friends? 'No,' came the reply, 'she's totally exhausted by the end of the week and often spends most of the weekend sleeping.' It was a comment rather than a criticism, but if that might apply to what's happening to you, then you need to find a fairer, better way to live. You can't expect to put children, parents, partner or friends 'on hold' for too long, or you may find you are no longer as important in their lives as you would like to be.

There are companies where the working culture is full on, virtually 24/7, but beware of the toll this will take on you and on those who are around you. One young woman in her first job was recently told that although she arrived at 8.30 am and left at 5.30 pm (her hours officially are 9 to 5), this was not sufficient, and she needed to spend more time at work. Certainly, we all have busy times, but this should be an occasional rather than a perpetual situation! Think about the following example:

> 'When I was offered the chance to create, from scratch, the unit I was thrilled, excited and totally overwhelmed. There and then, I was

determined that I would succeed – and I knew that it would not be easy although fortunately at that stage I did not appreciate just how difficult it would be. For two years, I worked most weekends and I often stayed during the week close to the office rather than taking the long train journey home. Holidays were impossible and I didn't want to take time away anyway, but now I can see that by the end of those two years I was completely drained, both physically and mentally. I thought that doing the job, and succeeding with it, was reward enough but I think it became an obsession ... It had to succeed and I thought that no-one else could possibly do what I did. I had a team to help me, and I could delegate to them, but I didn't – I felt driven totally by the scale of what I'd taken on.'

So, let's take a look at how you spend your time currently. The example pie chart below illustrates how you can divide the total area of 100 per cent into sections so you can review how you spend your time. In the example, we have used six different areas: 75 per cent work, 5 per cent social, 10 per cent family, 3 per cent volunteering, 5 per cent hobbies and 2 per cent 'me time'.

You may find you have either more or less in each section.

Life map

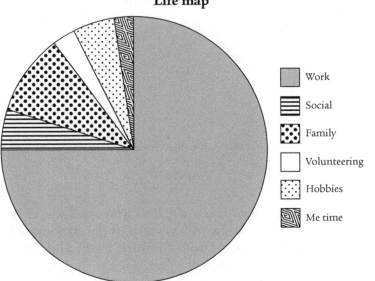

- Work
- Social
- Family
- Volunteering
- Hobbies
- Me time

Now draw your own life map describing how you currently spend your time. Use whatever headings are appropriate for you.

My current life map

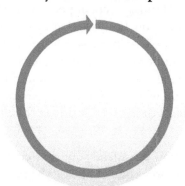

Now, just before you move on to think about your 'ideal' world, consider whether you have used the right headings above. In the 'ideal' map below, you may also include something new that isn't in your current timeline, or even remove something from the current map.

My ideal life map

Reflection. Consider what these two illustrations tell you about yourself – and please do be honest with yourself in the assessment process. Do you have separate compartments for work, leisure and family, or do they blend in together? There was a time, a few years ago, when people who owned a business might work evenings and weekends, but most workers stopped thinking about work after 5, 6 or 7 o'clock. These days, the lines between work and home are much more blurred, working hours are much longer in some professions, and more and more of us have what we might describe as a 'jigsaw life' in which we simply take our work and fit it into our family and personal holiday times. Many women struggle to keep everything going well and end up with no time for themselves. Being the perfect mother and perfect worker is invariably a tricky juggling act, so be careful that you are not trying to do too much in each part of your life. Be realistic rather than the impossible 'perfect' – as depicted in the Hollywood movie *I Don't Know How She Does It*.

You may also like to think about how you spend your time in relation to work by completing the short quiz below.

Statement	Yes, No, Sometimes	Observations
I generally work longer than forty hours each week.		
I generally work between forty and fifty hours each week.		
I generally work more than fifty hours each week.		
I generally work through my lunch break.		
I generally do not take all my holiday allowance.		
I generally take work home.		
I generally stay connected via mobile phone and email all the time.		
Are you happy about this? If not, what can you do about it?		

Technology should have helped us with these dilemmas, but it is clear that it has made our lives much worse in this regard; often in London restaurants (and no doubt in many other cities across the world) you will see couples out for a meal who are also using their phone, tablet or iPad to keep up to date with what's happening at work. As one senior woman manager (in retail) explained,

> 'how we deal with this I don't know. I have hardly any leisure time as I run my own business and my husband's calls for work begin at 7 a.m. in the morning and continue until he goes to bed. No wonder my daughters don't want the life that I have!'

It's easy to say that you need to work 'smarter' to deal with such issues. It's harder to do so, and many women we spoke to talk about how much harder it is for working mothers.

> 'I decided to go part-time, only 4 days a week, so that I can spend time with my daughter. Almost all of my friends have stayed full-time and are trying to manage the impossible. At least I can legitimately switch off my mobile but they can't and are expected by clients and the company to answer calls 24/7. I know I have gone down in terms of income and career prospects but I do feel I've made the right choice.'

Employers could, of course, do so much more to acknowledge these issues, create better policies and provide a more flexible system that builds part-time careers.

> 'My organization behaves as if every woman about to take maternity leave is the first time this has ever happened! And when she returns it's the same, everything here is a battle and organized on an ad hoc basis yet I know another similar company where it's a far more positive environment for working parents.'

Now that you have completed the reflections above, think about what you want from life in the comments box below. The results may not make for easy reading; we know from coaching sessions that if people feel trapped by work or family circumstances, they often suppress any thoughts about what they would really like to do. However, it's important for you to be honest about what's happening in your life. You do not necessarily have to change. The valuable aspect is to understand yourself better, and know what motivates and energizes you.

Complete the exercise below:

My current life versus my 'ideal' life:

What have I got that I want to keep:

What have I got that I want to change:

One action I could take to start this process of change – and when:

Another useful exercise below is to reflect on the people around you – on the left-hand side, list those who help you think about your career and what you want from your job. These are your positive supporters, admirers and helpers.

On the other, right-hand side are those who are not helping – they may be critical, or maybe you have a partner or family who try to put you off what you would like to do. One example from our survey is a partner who

'resented the times when I worked evenings and when I had to travel away from home.'

My career supporters – at work or at home	My career critics – at work or at home

Your reflections on the exercise above

Hopefully, that has helped you think about your current situation and what's happening for you. In the next section, we'll look more closely at where you are in your career.

Section 2: About your career

When you think about your career journey so far – whether you are at the start, in the middle or towards the end of your working life – it's also useful to think about what you enjoy about the work you do. Fill in the left-hand column (what you like) first and then consider what this tells you: for example, is it a long list or a short one? If it is a very short list, then maybe you are not in the right job for you? There may be other jobs that would be more fulfilling.

After you have spent some time on what you like, fill in the right-hand (what you dislike) column.

What I like about my job	Notes	What I dislike about my job	Notes

Many of the women we interviewed set out from the beginning knowing what they wanted to do – such as being an actress – but many of us 'fall' into that indeterminate place of 'undecided', or we float through life without any plan at all.

When we look at the past, we can see just how influential role models can be for women. If these do not exist in your organization – or in your sector – then it definitely makes younger women believe that it's likely to be harder to reach the top. Liz Bingham's comments in the *Guardian* – she is now a partner at Ernst & Young – make this point. She also highlights the multiple barriers women may face in modern-day careers.

One great role model example from the past is that of the cellist Jacqueline du Pré, who during the 1960s inspired a generation of younger women to take up classical music as a profession – something that had not previously happened. Virginia Wade, who won the women's tennis singles title at Wimbledon in 1977 – she also won Sports Personality of the Year in the BBC awards that same year – also enthused many younger women. And the American Chris Evert similarly inspired a generation of women in the 1990s. A modern equivalent would perhaps be Olympic Gold Medal winner Jessica Innes-Hill, orchestral conductor Marin Alsop or some CEOs, such as Kate Swann who was at WHSmith and Carolyn McCall at EasyJet.

Think about your own sector, or your part of the business, family members and friends and the women who are role models for you and your generation.

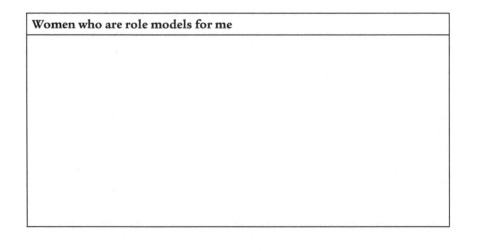

Women who are role models for me

You might also like to ask some of the people around you – those whom you know well and feel that you can trust. Maybe you have a boss from a previous company, your partner, or a friend who has been close to you over the years as you have worked in different jobs. You can also try to answer these questions about yourself.

- Am I in the right place/job/role/sector/company?
- How do others see me – for example, do I have a reputation as someone who works hard and adds value?
- What are my weaknesses, and do these matter?
- What are my strengths, and do I make the most of these?
- What do you think I could achieve if I set my mind on it?

Section 3: Career choices you may face

One of the interesting points about career choices, or maybe we should call them crossroads or life stages, is that often it is easier for someone else to recognize them than it is for ourselves. Perhaps the story below will help illustrate this point:

> 'I've often coached other women in my organization. I was involved in setting up a development programme and I'm really interested in the power of coaching. I can often see when women have reached a key point in their career for example, they have 4 or 5 years of good project experience, they have had a stint as a team leader and could stay where they are and get even more experience but ... I know that the next few years spent in a different place in the company, say on an international assignment, will really add value to their CV and make a big difference to their career potential.'

Of course, in some companies, this kind of advice and support is available, and we did hear a few examples of this from respondents to our survey. However, we were hardly overwhelmed with such stories, and this clearly is an area where employers could provide much more support and advice for women. There will be many younger women who should be able to see this 'bigger picture' in order to develop the right CV, but they need advice from others who have more experience in different parts of the business. This is where in-house women's networks can be so valuable. You meet people at different career stages from around the company and can therefore begin to appreciate what's required to 'get on around here'.

The following exercises are designed to help you reflect on your career. The first one deals with the current situation, but the second – and perhaps the most important aspect – is looking forward a few years.

My current career

Where I am now	Some of the career choices I have made to get to this point (and how these have helped me)

My future career

Where I would like to be five years from now	Some of the career choices I could make to get to this point (and how these would help me)

You can also carry out a similar review if you prefer to use life stages – as shown below.

My career

Where I am now and career choices I made to get to this point	Career choices I could make to get further (and how these would help me)
Early career: Millennials and generation Y, 20s–30s	
Mid-career: 30s–40s	
Mature career: Baby boomers, 50s–60+	

Take one of these choices – perhaps a recent event so that everything is fresh in your mind – and consider what happened:

- What was the dilemma you faced, and why was it important?
- Who else was affected by your decision – partner, family, colleagues, etc.?
- Who gave you advice and support during this time?
- What are the insights (or learning) you can take from this – think about the short term as well as those for the longer term?

Another way of learning about yourself, and your values, is to consider career setbacks that you have experienced. They often reveal a good deal about us – a bad situation can sometimes make us stronger, more determined and more resilient, or we find other qualities that we didn't realize we had. A recent magazine article asked a number of famous women about what had happened to them, and what they had learnt from the experience. As shown in the two examples below, it is possible to gain something good from what seems at the time to be a very bad experience. By the way, we also notice in our coaching that the ability to learn from a bad experience is a valuable skill to learn, as this helps you move forward in your life.

Get bullied – and come back stronger Jude Kelly, artistic director, Southbank Centre. Jude confronted the situation that had happened to her when she already held a senior appointment. There is an assumption that bullying only happens to people at a junior level. It can happen in any part of your career; someone who replied to our survey highlighted something similar when she was already a director in the public sector. 'It took me a while to realise what was happening but then when I moved to another boss who behaved in a similar way I knew straight away what was going on.'

'Feel out of your depth' was the advice offered by Jay Hunt, chief creative officer, Channel 4. It's not what you might expect but there is an important learning point from this. At the age of 22, Jay was in the newsroom as a junior player. However, a new editor who knew nothing about her background gave her a great opportunity – to be out of her depth – and although it was scary she did it well – 'There's nothing more empowering than someone believing you can do something, even if **you** don't believe you can do it.'

Examples of career crossroads
The examples below are taken from our survey and illustrate a number of key issues. You might like to consider whether any of these apply to you at the moment – they include:

- Whether or not to apply for a promotion.
- Your first team leadership opportunity.
- An international assignment.
- Working with someone whom you admire.
- The first five years of your career.

- Being offered a new opportunity out of your comfort zone.
- Reaching a career plateau: there are many times when your career may plateau or stagnate, and you may need to reinvent yourself or look at different roles in other sectors. However, one woman, who is an actress, said:

> 'I can't imagine anyone stuck in the acting profession mid-career, the business doesn't hold on to you that tightly to get stuck. My advice would be not to let it be everything. If you are lucky you can do other things associated with acting such as choreography, corporate acting, directing, producing, writing, all of which keep your skills honed and you part of the world, because the world is your workshop. Even the most employed actors do other things. Don't sit at home on your own waiting; as in that route madness lies! If you are a woman of a certain age, be comforted that a lot of the competition have dropped out by now. It is a very hard career to sustain. When you are on tour, it is not conducive to family life or any sort of life. The costs are high with very little structured support. It is a rubbish career. It is a wonderful career. I have no regrets.'

Finding your way in such a sector, or a profession that is so competitive, can be equally tough and rewarding. The important point, perhaps, is to understand just how much resilience you may need for a career in many areas: for example, in law, journalism, modelling, acting, publishing and academic life. Never underestimate just how much stick-ability you need to stay in the career you choose. There is often a good deal written about how hard it is to be an entrepreneur – and it is true – but we also heard a good deal in our interviews and in the survey about the difficult, hard times of maintaining a career in a numerous different environments, sectors, organizations, professions and industries.

Section 4: Career challenges women have faced and ways to overcome such challenges

There are so many inspiring stories that it's difficult to know which ones to select. A recent book by Azi Ahmed, for example, highlights her journey of leaving the traditional Pakistani role her family wished for her, via the army as a recruit for the SAS, to being a school governor and parliamentary candidate for Rochdale. This was the first group of women to join the SAS, so perhaps both sides felt nervous! A number of the women we interviewed for this book illustrate determination and focus in so many different ways. The first, who is now back working in the UK, has had five major career changes in her life, working in Greece and Brussels, and has been an entrepreneur with her own successful training company.

One woman whom we interviewed for this book is now a freelance director of photography, and knew from the age of fifteen that she wanted to be involved in films. However, she has followed an unconventional, if not unique, path that has included time as a building site labourer as well as a stint as a lecturer.

This chapter has tried to offer you a review of your current career – a more detailed career audit can be found in Chapter 1. Together, they offer you different perspectives – for example, look at the career stages shown below and consider your own situation.

Different generations and women's careers

Life and career stages	Age	Career issues for women
The **'baby boomers'** were born up to the early 1960s (the name comes from the situation – when the birth rate increased). In the United States and Europe, this group often think of themselves as special – different from the previous generation – as they benefitted from the post-war boom and new freedoms. **(36% of the UK workforce)** Many baby boomers joined company graduate schemes: Unilever, Macmillan Press, BT and Marks & Spencer all had programmes. There was a good deal of loyalty between workers and their company.	Over 55	Limited career opportunities existed for many women of this generation: clerical and office work, teaching and nursing were the usual jobs. Few women aspired to be managers, and many gave up work when they had children. The 'trailing spouse' was a term given to women who followed the moves made by their husband.

Life and career stages	Age	Career issues for women
'Generation X' (Gen X) are the following generation, born from the early 1960s to the early 1980s. Having seen what happened to their parents in the 1980s, losing their jobs through redundancy and downsizing, they see careers differently. They tend to change jobs regularly and are far less 'loyal'. They have high expectations of promotion and/or move frequently because they get bored. Many Gen-Xers have not experienced job security, so their approach is more transactional: jobs are simply stepping stones to other places. Did they invent the 'Gap Year'? Probably, as this term was first used in the 1970s for the time taken after university and before starting work, usually for a year to travel. **(35% of the workforce)**	35–55	Greater career opportunities for women. Work–life balance is important. Dual-career couples become more common.
'Generation Y' or Millennials, born from the early 1980s to the early 2000s, so some are still joining the workforce. Known as the 'techie generation', they are likely to make up almost half the working population by 2020. Where baby boomers prefer 'face to face time', Gen Y prefer email, instant messaging (IM) and Facebook, rather than talking on the phone or face-to-face. Gen Y seek personal growth and interesting careers. However, they don't tend to stay in one job for very long – often only up to two years – and many are interested in taking time out for travelling or other personal development pursuits.	15–35	This generation have benefitted from having baby boomer parents, many of whom were pioneers as dual-career couples. It is also worth saying that a major learning from their baby boomer parents is the importance of work–life balance (for both men and women). The women of this generation have more career opportunities, more independence and more choice than any previous generation. Yet, the pay gap and many inequalities in the workplace still exist between men and women.

Life and career stages	Age	Career issues for women
This means that turnover levels for Gen Y staff can be higher than for other age groups. **(20% of the workforce)**		It hasn't all been plain sailing, though. The GenY-ers leaving school and those graduating from 2007 onwards have had to deal with living through one of the worst economic recessions since the 1930s. This has had a significant effect on ability to find jobs and thus their loyalty to organizations.
'Generation Z', born since the mid-2000s and still in education, but the next generation of the workforce	Up to 10 years old	Difficult to say as yet.

It's also worth thinking about what your advice would be to your younger self – you may only be in your 20s now, but often we learn a lot quite quickly about our working life. One of the survey respondents – someone in her 30s who is running her own company – said:

'Do the same as you have done, in particular:

- be positive and optimistic

- be passionate about what you are doing

- do things (do not be afraid about making mistakes)

- be ready to do something risky, even if the chances for success look 5%.'

Another woman in her 40s who replied has an international career with a multinational:

'I would say I should vocalize my own expectations: clearly and constructively. And certainly to get a mentor – don't be shy to ask for help and advice at any stage!'

Summary

We hope that you can now see some career goals. Ask yourself: can you see some immediate job changes that would improve your working life and your personal life? See the career resources section below for some more suggestions. Can you also see some longer-term career goals?

Do you have a realistic view of the career you want? For example, you may dream about being an actress, but one of the facts you need to know is that there is something like 90 per cent unemployment in this profession – and even many successful actors struggle to find their next role in theatre, film or TV. It's very tough.

Music, modelling or journalism are also notoriously difficult places to build a career. Georgia May Jagger (daughter of Mick Jagger and Jerry Hall), for example, started modelling in 2008, and in 2009 won 'Model of the Year' at the British Fashion Awards, but there will be many, many others who started modelling at the same time as she did who were not as fortunate.

And finally, in this chapter, a word about opportunities. If you are offered an opportunity, then do please think about it, consider all the reasons why you **should** take it and then seize it. Women often have the opposite tendency – to think about all the reasons why **they can't do something.** Beware of falling into that 'negative thinking' trap that can be so destructive.

- One woman we met told us her story. She had all the skills and passion to start her own business – as a personal trainer – but feels more comfortable staying with her full-time job working at something she doesn't like. You might say this could be a commonsense, cautious choice she is making, why lose a salary and risk starting your own company? But, there are lots of in-between options such as using every Saturday to try out business ideas and to build a customer base. Start up an evening class with a similar motive to see if it will appeal to people. Another might be to find a friend with similar ideas and work together ... and there are others.

Be ambitious and, of course, do remember the value of doing your homework and making sure you are well informed for any meetings, pitches or interviews. Someone who was offered an interview unexpectedly at a major company spent all the time she had until the interview learning about the company:

'I didn't know at that point whether or not I wanted the job but I did know that I wanted to impress them at the interview. I read everything about the company that I could find so that I knew as much as possible about them.'

The list below is a sample of some of the wide range of resources available to help you – undoubtedly there are many other resources; we simply wanted to highlight the sort of help available to you.

Career resources:

Green Careers for Dummies by Carol McClelland, 2010, Wiley Publishing.

Banking & Investments Career Guide 2014/15, 12th edition, edited by Michael Hennessy, Inside Careers, www.insidecareers.co.uk.

The Great Mid-Life Career Switch: 15 Important Tips to Help You Change Careers at Half-Time by Gordon Adams, 2010, Infinite Ideas Ltd.

Becoming a Personal Trainer for Dummies by Melyssa St. Michael and Linda Formichelli, 2004, Wiley Publishing.

Vault Guide to the Top 50 Accounting Firms, 2016 edition by Derek Loosvelt, 2015, www.vault.com.

If you are interested in a career as a developer in a start-up business, look at www.workshape.io, an online talent-matching company for techie start-ups.

The Times Top 50 Employers for Women 2013, see Opportunity Now website link: http://opportunitynow.bitc.org.uk.

How to become a doctor: see British Medical Association website link http://bma.org.uk.

If you are interested in developing a career as a hospital doctor or GP, be aware that it is likely to be a long haul and involve a minimum of five years at university, followed by several more years of practical training.

How to Get a Career in Retailing: see the *Guardian* website link: www.theguardian.com.

And don't forget to check out professional associations such as the CIPD (for HR practitioners) and search for others, such as those noted below. All are likely to have career advice and events that will be helpful for you. RIBA, the Royal Institute for British Architecture, is based in London and holds many meetings and events for members. See www.architecture.com/Explore/Home.aspx.

It's always worthwhile searching for articles or books that might help you – for example, Adrian Dobson, a director at RIBA, published a book in 2014 entitled *21 Things You Won't Learn in Architecture School*.

Someone who's interested to find out about psychology as a career, for example, could:

1. Review friends and colleagues, and ask about friends of friends.
2. Find out which are the best universities for psychology. There are lots of different fields you could work in, such as social work, child development, mental health and occupational psychology, which all bring different career possibilities and different working environments.
3. Look at the resources available from the professional body, the BPS (the British Psychological Society). There will be events for students, an annual general conference as well as specialist conferences such as the annual conference for occupational psychology, and career information. See http://careers.bps.org.uk.

The Law Society has a 'Women Lawyers Division' with free resources and events. It also offers courses to help 'returners', those who have taken time away and now want to rejoin the profession, and there are also regional groups, for example in Bristol, offering local support. See http://communities.lawsociety.org.uk.

Women in Advertising: www.adwomen.org.

Medical Women's Federation: www.medicalwomensfederation.org.uk.

Women in Film and Television UK: www.wftv.org.uk.

If you belong to any women's networks, you should be able to find similar resources.

MindTools.Com is an online resource that teaches you over 1,000 skills that help you to excel at work. Try searching their website at www.mindtools.com.

TED Talks is an excellent online resource that promotes ideas worth spreading. Have a look at www.ted.com/talks.

Skills You Need is a website run by a group of lifelong learners who are sharing their knowledge and expertise to help others. Have a look at www.skillsyouneed.com.

Remember, most importantly ...

... it's never, NEVER, too late to change your career or to decide that you've been on the wrong path. We know of someone in her 40s who moved from a corporate career to a senior role in the National Trust, and other career-changers include:

- Someone who recently set up her own floristry business – and learnt everything she needed to know about flowers from watching YouTube videos.
- Another woman we know who moved from marketing expert to language teacher, and now, in her 50s, is working on her third career, weaving and dyeing her own fabrics to use in making exclusive hats, bags and jewellery. She's just taken up spinning as well.
- The recently appointed female Bishop of Gloucester (Rachel Treweek) started her working career as a speech therapist and worked in the NHS for six years before retraining as a vicar.

Chapter 4

Essential skills and qualities for career success

One of the areas that many of the women we interviewed and surveyed talked about was having the right range of skills and qualities for success in their particular business area.

We have identified a range of different skills and qualities that seem to contribute to an individual's success at work. Obviously, this is not an exhaustive list; however, it is based on what many working women tell us and what we hear from people during our research, coaching, teaching and consulting assignments.

We have split the skills and qualities into four main areas:

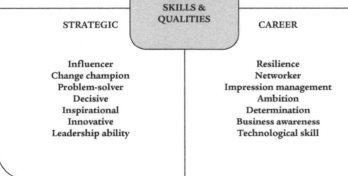

PERSONAL

Self-confidence
Initiative
Results oriented
Flexible
Collaborative
Self-belief
Emotional awareness
Deals with ambiguity
Articulate

RELATIONSHIP

Interpersonal skill
Develops others
Motivates others
Builds relationships
Teamworker
Deals with conflict

ESSENTIAL SKILLS & QUALITIES

STRATEGIC

Influencer
Change champion
Problem-solver
Decisive
Inspirational
Innovative
Leadership ability

CAREER

Resilience
Networker
Impression management
Ambition
Determination
Business awareness
Technological skill

In the chapters that follow, we will look at each of the four main areas – Personal, Relationship, Strategic and Career – and then make a detailed examination of each of the individual skills and qualities. We will describe what contributes to success and make suggestions for developing your ability in the skill or quality.

You might find it useful to refer back to the Skills and Quality Audit that featured in Chapter 1 before you start reading through the following four chapters. This will enable you to structure your reading around those skills and qualities that will be most useful for your development or that interest you the most. Remember, your development is about your current needs as well as those skills and qualities you will require to progress in your career.

For example, examine your completed skills and qualities audit in Chapter 1, and you will find it most beneficial to focus on those skills and qualities that you have highlighted as development areas. This means that to get the best from the following four chapters you will only focus on certain topics in each chapter.

Our advice would be to focus on those areas that you believe to be of significant importance to you and your success – don't try to tackle too many.

Chapter 5

Essential personal skills and qualities

We have identified nine personal skills and qualities that we believe make a difference to your day-to-day working life and will contribute to your career success. Many of these personal skills and qualities overlap with each other, so working to develop even a few of them will contribute to building your ability in others.

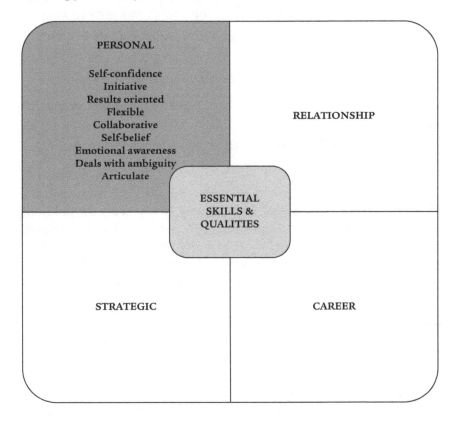

PERSONAL

Self-confidence
Initiative
Results oriented
Flexible
Collaborative
Self-belief
Emotional awareness
Deals with ambiguity
Articulate

RELATIONSHIP

ESSENTIAL SKILLS & QUALITIES

STRATEGIC

CAREER

Personal skills and qualities

- **Self-confidence** is the capability that is mentioned most frequently by women in our research as the area they most need to develop, and above all else, it is probably the single most important ability for success in many aspects of our lives.

Here's a sample of some of the comments made. First, when asked about barriers, respondents said:

'One of my biggest barriers was my own self-limiting beliefs and confidence.'

'Losing self confidence has been the biggest barrier in my working life. I had it in abundance in my twenties, but somehow it slipped away.'

'Most barriers I've faced have been around self confidence and finding my voice.'

When asked about advice they'd give their younger self, they said:

'Don't let self confidence hold you back – give it a go, no matter whether you fail or succeed!'

'Be confident, believe in yourself, this helps others to believe in you.'

'Don't worry so much, be confident.'

Outwardly, self-confidence is demonstrated by the behaviour you use when interacting with others – what you say, how you say it, your body language and the overall impression you have on others. However, being self-confident is rather more complex than simply using behaviour that leaves others with the right impression. To be truly self-confident, you must demonstrate it to the outside world **and** feel it for yourself.

Some people are self-confident in some situations while finding it difficult to demonstrate in others. For instance, we often hear from people that they are self-confident when interacting with family, friends and close colleagues, but when they have to communicate with people not so well known to them, they find it much more difficult to be confident – these people could be clients, bosses, customers or more senior colleagues. For others, it is not the people but the situation they face: for instance, when presenting to a group, when speaking at a conference, when meeting someone new for the first time, or even when trying to get heard at a meeting. Whatever the situation, it is possible to improve your confidence.

Building your confidence

Positive inner voice + Planning & preparation + Skill development + Having a supporter = CONFIDENCE

Developing and demonstrating self-confidence is often largely about your own attitudes: being aware of your strengths and weaknesses (see the SWOT Analysis Exercise in Chapter 1) so that you can demonstrate and capitalize on your strengths while also finding ways to develop your weaknesses, and operating from an optimistic frame of mind where you avoid negative self-talk, which tends to be toxic and demoralizing. For instance, having an inner dialogue with yourself that sows seeds of doubt in your mind about your ability will affect your internal and external self-confidence. Far better to develop internal self-dialogue telling yourself things such as:

'I can do this, I have the skills and abilities' or 'I am going to give this a go, what's the worst that can happen?'

Working from a positive mindset takes practice and determination, but will pay dividends in the long run.

There are three additional important influences for self-confidence. First is your ability to plan and prepare for the various situations you face in your life and career. It is probably impossible to prepare for every eventuality, but if you are aware of the main challenges you have with self-confidence, then you can mitigate them by focusing on planning and preparation. Second is knowledge and skill development: taking the opportunity to develop your knowledge and skill base in areas where you know you are weak will lead to far greater self-confidence. Third, you may like to think about having a supporter in the early days of trying out anything new. This person can be there to encourage you, give you feedback and even provide a safety net should things go wrong.

In our survey, many women indicated that investing in their own development was a major boost to their confidence, for instance:

'I was sponsored by my organization to do an MBA which has been a massive boost to my confidence.'

'I just focused on developing my skillsets and taking up as many learning opportunities as possible.'

Reflection. You may like to think about key situations you face in your career or life: for instance, meeting new people, chairing a meeting, making a presentation, managing a difficult situation, taking on new responsibility, dealing with senior people, expressing yourself in public, influencing others, saying no, dealing with ambiguous situations, etc. If confidence is an issue for you, you will find it helpful to work with a coach, mentor or support network. By doing this, you will be able to work together to identify practical and realistic ways of improving.

One amazing woman who understood the importance of confidence for women was Stephanie Fierz, who was headmistress of a girls' school for nineteen years. One of her pupils, Claudia Rosencrantz (creator of the TV programme *I'm a Celebrity* ...), said of her:

'You marinated us all in confidence, and you accepted each one of us just as we were ....'

A recent book by Kay and Shipman called *The Confidence Code: The Science and Art of Self Assurance – What Women Should Know* explores this area in more detail.

- **Uses initiative**

  Initiative is all about being an independent self-starter who takes action to make things happen to achieve goals. Being proactive and taking control of any situation will set you apart from the norm, and doing this with you own career management will only pay dividends in the long run.

  People who use their initiative will tend to take action without being told to and come up with original and new ideas for solving problems and challenges. They tend to do more than is required of them, often taking on additional responsibilities to help develop their career and increase their visibility. Initiators will always seek out the next interesting opportunity and will ask themselves how they can best capitalize on any situation to learn and develop.

For instance, in one of our interviews with a woman who is a senior organization development professional in the NHS, she talked about being competitive with herself. This led her to

'use her initiative to set things up',

always seeking out possibilities to get involved in high-profile projects and learning and development events, all of which would improve her visibility in the organization and ultimately improve her career development prospects. Such opportunities include taking part in Operation Raleigh, setting up and running development events for colleagues, sending her CV speculatively to possible employers, and reaching out to her contacts to help her find new career opportunities.

Certain personal characteristics can be attached to people who use their initiative, including:

- self-confident
- tenacious and determined
- articulate and passionate
- inquiring and curious
- independent
- development oriented
- resilient

Many of the women who responded to our survey mentioned initiative as one of the main areas they have had to demonstrate to manage their career and achieve their ambitions.

Some of the things they say are:

'being a challenger and having a clear path and vision'

'showing dedication, confidence and taking responsibility which can slowly change others' mindsets'

'sheer determination and delivery over and above goals'

Ability to use initiative is one of the key characteristics many employers seek today, so time spent working on the characteristics mentioned earlier will be valuable for your future success. It is particularly valued by employers today, because in our ever-increasingly competitive and technological world they need people who are willing to work independently, think on their feet and deal with tricky situations without waiting for instruction from others.

Reflection. You might also like to reflect about your current ability in this area and plan how you can demonstrate and use your initiative in your current role. Use the following questions as a prompt.

Use of initiative – Personal review

QUESTION	NOTES
In my career so far, when have I used my initiative?	
What opportunities have I taken in recent years to demonstrate initiative in my job?	
Thinking about a time when I have used my initiative, what skills and abilities did I use?	
Does your organization (or boss) actively encourage you to use your initiative? If not, why not?	
On a scale of 1 to 10, how confident am I about using my initiative in my current role? Why is this?	
What recognition have I had for using my initiative?	
What more could I do to demonstrate initiative? What steps can I take now?	

- **Results oriented**

People who are results oriented are committed to delivering on objectives and goals, meeting deadlines and ensuring projects they are involved in are seen through to completion. They will overcome obstacles, work with others and ensure that business objectives are met.

Most employers are recognizing that it is the focus on results that drives business success, rather than working long hours and simply being present. Many people now work 'from home' or 'virtually', so there is a greater realization that results orientation is a key competence for success. For individuals, this means knowing what's expected of you, prioritizing and organizing to ensure you can achieve your goals and objectives on time and to the agreed quality.

More than this, it is also important to share your results with others to help promote your capabilities and success. Being results-focused is only one aspect of this capability; you must also be willing to promote your results as your achievements. Many women mentioned this aspect of their working life as a barrier to their success, especially when they were not actively recognized for their achievements and results.

Some of the things our respondents said were:

'I had difficulties in promotion in terms of recognition of research achievements. Passed over in favour of candidates with less funding and less prestigious publications. Solved by moving to another institution'

'Staying too long in a company progressing from a junior in HR to a Senior Manager yet still being regarded by some as a "green graddy" and not being given the respect earned for the results achieved'

'Not being sufficiently loud about my successes early on, seeing others (mainly men) being promoted before/above me. I started mentioning areas of my job that I had done well to senior management when in general conversations and updates meetings with them. I no longer assume they will simply notice the brilliant job I am doing.'

We suspect that many women are particularly good at being results oriented; you have told us in both the interviews and the survey that in order to get good balance and to meet the multiple demands on your time, prioritizing, being organized and results-focused are all major components of both your working and your personal life. The problem for many seems to be letting others know about these successes in an effective way, without being regarded as boastful or arrogant. So, rather than waiting for people to simply recognize your achievements, it might be worth thinking about how you can promote your achievements effectively. For instance, during performance reviews, talk about not only results but also the impact of these results. Similarly, when preparing a CV, make sure you promote your achievements quite clearly.

Reflection. You might find it useful to reflect about how you keep the people in your network up to date about your results and achievements. Should you be doing more of this? Are you satisfied with the level of recognition you get for your results? If not, what more can you do to ensure others are aware of your results and achievements?

While all of this is important when being results oriented, it is also vital to remember that you must not forget about maintaining and building your relationship focus as well, and ensuring that both your staff and your bosses are kept informed of objectives and targets.

- **Flexibility**

Flexibility is about being adaptable to different situations, work styles and patterns of behaviour. Change is inevitable, so being flexible in the way you work will help you to work and succeed in today's business environment.

Flexibility demands that you are willing to adapt your own attitudes and behaviours to best manage any situation and the people involved in it. If you demonstrate adaptability, you will have to use good communication skills, using inquiry to explore ideas with others, listening actively to their point of view, and demonstrating that you have adapted and learnt new ways of doing things. This will help to make you a valuable commodity in this world, where many people find change difficult to cope with, are often rigid in their ways of operating and won't try out new ideas.

It is also worth noting that sometimes women feel that they are being too accommodating and flexible with others. The trick is to get the balance right.

Reflection. You may like to use the quiz below to assess your ability to flex and adapt.

Flexibility quiz

Look at the questions below and rate yourself on a scale of 1 (not very) to 5 (always), then make notes about why you have scored the way you have.		
Question	**Score**	**Notes**
I easily adapt to changing situations and environments		
I am always receptive to others' ideas and views		
I am happy to take on new challenges at short notice		
I like learning new skills and techniques		
I like to keep an open mind		
I like juggling different projects and multitasking		
I am excited by the challenge of change		
I flex my approach to others to accommodate their behaviour and way of working		
Looking at your answers, what does this tell you about your approach to flexibility and adaptability? Make notes below.		

Flexibility is more of an attitude of mind than a skill, and there are a few things you can do to develop and demonstrate that you are adaptable to change and flex. These include:

- Showing a willingness to try out new ways of doing things and take on new tasks and projects.
- When you are operating in an environment that is changing, demonstrate that you are exploring ways of making the changes work rather than simply complaining about the change.
- Be prepared to move away from an established, preset plan to accommodate new information or ideas.
- Show resilience and a positive attitude to dealing with the unexpected.

- **Collaboration**

  Being collaborative is all about working with others in a partnership to accomplish a common goal. True collaborators demonstrate an ability to pursue team goals as well as personal goals. It is about not just listening to others but really hearing what others say and then working with them to reach a mutually acceptable outcome. Typically, people who collaborate well enjoy teamwork, developing relationships and working with others.

  Your tendency towards collaborative working can be environmental – by this we mean that certain national cultures and organizational cultures are more likely to work in a collaborative way than others, and therefore this may affect an individual's preferences and abilities. Of course, they may also be affected by your personality. That said, it is possible to learn and develop collaborative working skills and processes.

  Some of the key features and skills demonstrated by people who have a preference for collaboration include:

  - Using inquiry and questioning others to ascertain their perspectives on various issues that you collectively are dealing with.
  - Actively listening to what others have to say and engaging in a dialogue to explore and work things through together.
  - Being willing to admit that you do not have all the answers – you may have a perspective on an issue, but you also realize that others, too, will have ideas. Adopting approaches such as brainstorming and other creative problem-solving and teamworking processes.
  - Keeping people up to date by sharing information with others – recognizing that knowledge and information help people to perform

to their best ability, so share what you know with others rather than hoarding information to enhance your status.

One collaborative technique we have found very useful in our work as consultants is applying the following process when we are meeting with others to explore a problem with them to agree a way ahead or plan of action.

A process for collaborative working and problem-solving

- Stage 1 – Prior to the meeting, make all attendees (usually this process works best with up to eight people) aware of the issue under discussion. State this clearly and succinctly. For instance, 'The purpose of the meeting is to develop ideas and agree proposals to put to the management board about appropriate performance measures for managers and staff.'
- Stage 2 – Make everyone aware that they will all be asked to bring along their own ideas and be willing to share them in the group.
- Stage 3 – The meeting
  - Restate the purpose and remind people of the time available – again, clearly and succinctly; maybe have it visible on a whiteboard or screen.
  - Split the time available into three parts and allocate time appropriately (for instance, if you have two hours, you might spend forty minutes in individual sharing, fifty minutes in discussion and thirty minutes agreeing the action plan) – part one, individual sharing; part two, discussion; and part three, agreeing the way ahead/action plan.
  - During this process, there are two roles to be played. The coordinator ensures everyone obeys the rules (e.g. speaking for a maximum of five minutes, with no one interrupting). The second role is that of the scribe – either an external facilitator or one of the group who will make brief notes of each person's ideas. It is usually best if these notes are visible to everyone during the process, so it may be a good idea to use a whiteboard or flipchart paper.
  - In part one, each person is allocated a time slot. For instance, with eight people and forty minutes in total, each person would be given five minutes. During this time, each person states his or her perspective and ideas without interruption or questions. The scribe makes brief notes of each person's key ideas.

○ In part two, the coordinator (or project leader) summarizes what has been shared so far (at this stage, we often find that there is much in common, which means that you can focus on the differences rather than spending time on things you already agree) and then manages a group discussion to explore the areas where there is some disagreement or variation in views. During this process, good interactive processes are applied – questioning, listening (uninterrupted), summarizing and testing for understanding.

○ In part three, the project leader will summarize what has been agreed through this process. At this stage, if people have agreed to do further work on the issue, then in order to gain their commitment to action and ensure that everyone is in agreement, each person should be asked to state what they will do and by when. This verbal statement ensures that everything is in the open and shared.

○ A final stage after the meeting may be to send meeting notes to all involved, summarizing what was agreed and the way ahead.

This type of collaborative process has significant benefits in that everyone has an opportunity to share their ideas in an open forum, and no one person gets longer airtime than others – this is particularly good for the quieter members of any group, or in groups where different organizational levels are represented. Using this type of technique demonstrates that you are willing to listen to others and take their ideas on board, and by modelling this you will be encouraging others to use collaborative processes.

Techniques such as this are useful in many situations, but not necessarily all situations. It is also worth stating that, even in using this type of collaborative process, there comes a time when someone or a small group has to take responsibility and manage the way ahead. The true benefit, though, is that you have a group of people who have worked with you and who feel you have listened to them and worked collaboratively.

Reflection. Assess your own skill in this area by completing the quiz below.

Quiz – How collaborative are you?

Look at each of the statements below and assess your own skill and ability in the area. Score yourself on a scale of 1 to 5, from 1 being not skilled to 5 being highly skilled.

STATEMENT	SCORE
I easily create rapport with others	
I listen actively to others	
I encourage cooperative behaviours from colleagues and team members	
I work towards getting 'buy in' from others	
I like involving others	
I build consensus and work towards mutually acceptable outcomes	
I recognize and value others' contributions	
I seek to create common ground	
I encourage sharing and dialogue between myself and team members	
I am curious to know others' perspective on issues	

Summary. Looking at the scores, the more 4s and 5s you have scored, the more collaborative you are. You may also like to use the space below to make any notes about developing your collaborative skills.

- **Self-belief**

  Together with confidence, this is the capability most mentioned by our respondents and interviewees as the area that causes them most problems. Some women talk about simply not having belief in their own abilities – often

  'waiting to be found out'.

Others say that experiences at work (or even in life) have an effect on chipping away at their self-belief.

'One of my biggest barriers was my own self limiting beliefs. I have constantly had to work at this through my working life.'

'My own belief and doubt in my ability to contribute at a senior level and a conservatism about applying for senior jobs. (Overcome by applying and getting a senior job).'

'A lack of self belief, being too risk averse in career decisions'

'Toxic self-talk that has led me to doubt myself and either not speak up, not push myself forward, even tell people that I am not good enough for an opportunity they offered me'

However, in addition to these negative comments, many also believe that

'Self belief is (one of) the most powerful ingredients in getting a job.'

If you are one of these people who have low self-belief or who struggle at times with self-belief issues, you are not alone, and it's an area that can be worked on and developed.

So, what is self-belief? The dictionary says: 'confidence in oneself and one's ability'. Largely, self-belief comes from within us. We all have the ability to have self-belief, but it can take a bit of work, a change in attitude and focus. One of the first things to do is to understand why your self-belief is low. In our survey we heard lots of reasons, including:

- poor education
- various issues around upbringing
- discrimination at work
- being turned down for promotion
- being made redundant
- lack of positive feedback at home or at work
- a combination of different issues involving a series of knocks at work and at home

Understanding the root cause of your self-belief issues will help you to overcome them and work to improve.

Some of the things you can do to change your attitude to yourself and develop self-belief include:

- **Controlling your negative self-talk**, those thoughts you have about yourself that can turn into toxic self-talk and will send you into a downward spiral. So, instead of focusing on the negative, why not think about the positive? Maybe make a list of all the things you have achieved during the course of this year/decade or all the great things that have happened to you – whatever works best for you. Changing your mindset is the first step to improved self-belief. So, focus on the positive.
- **Focus on the people in your life** – all of them – family, friends and colleagues. Who are the people who support and help you, and who are the ones who drag you down, the glass-half-empty people? Be aware of who energizes you and avoid the energy sappers.
- **Set goals**. There is nothing quite as rewarding and boosting as achieving a goal, especially one of these goals we all think we can't achieve – maybe a sporting one, such as running a half marathon, or a working one, such as applying for and getting promotion. For us, it was writing a book and getting it published. Achieving your goals and focusing on how you did it will help enormously in building self-belief.

As Jennifer Capriati said,

'Dreams do come true if you keep believing in yourself. Anything is possible',

and as Bear Grylls said,

'The special forces gave me the self confidence to do some extraordinary things in my life. Climbing Everest then cemented my belief in myself'

Now, we can't all become champion tennis players or mountain climbers, but we can all set goals for ourselves and achieve them. It is also often worth starting small: set small steps, as each small win is reinforcing.

- **Think about the impression you are creating**. When you meet and greet people, what do you say, how do you say it, what do your body language and facial impression imply? Looking and sounding confident will affect the way others react to us and, in turn, will affect our own confidence levels and self-belief. Here are some tips when you meet and greet people:

- Facial expression – smiling when you first meet people implies confidence and success, and is easier than frowning!
- Think about your posture – stand up straight with your shoulders back.
- Look at the person – make eye contact.
- Dress appropriately and comfortably.
- If shaking hands (yes, we know it's a bit of a cliché), remember a firm clasp of hands, not a bone breaker or a wet limp fish!
- Plan what you might say so that you are able to begin a conversation.
- Ask others about your 'image'. Sometimes it is surprising to discover the gap between how we see ourselves and how others see us.

Some of these tips apply to many interpersonal situations. The important issue is to always be aware of the impression you are creating, as this will affect the way that others treat you and, in turn, that will affect how you feel about yourself.

Remember, working on your self-belief requires effort and focus; it can be a challenge, and no one else can do it for you.

Reflection. How would you score yourself in relation to self-belief – let's say 1 means very low and completely lacking, and 10 means extremely high, not a problem. If it's low, set yourself a goal of, say, moving from 3 to 5 – what can you do, how will you do it and on what timescale? Remember, one of the key challenges is to have goals and achievements and celebrate them. By using small steps to improve, you are more likely to achieve and build your self-belief as you go.

- **Emotional awareness**

This is about recognizing both your own emotional state and that of others. It is also about being able to discriminate between different feelings and how they affect behaviour. Emotional awareness is more than simply having good communication skills; it is about:

- Recognizing your own emotions and how they affect your thoughts and behaviour.
- Understanding what your emotions are telling you and reacting appropriately for the situation.

- Being aware of your emotional 'triggers' and how to manage these to ensure effective outcomes and good-quality relationships.
- Recognizing how your emotions affect the people you interact with.
- Responding to and recognizing others' emotions.
- Having the ability to develop and maintain healthy, good-quality relationships in all aspects of your life.

Reflection. There are some simple things you can do to assess your emotional intelligence and also to develop your ability in this area. The following short exercise will help you assess your own.

Read the statement in the table below and assess your capability. If you feel you need to develop your emotional awareness, you could try out some of the ideas that follow.

Emotional awareness quiz

	Indicate your capability Yes/No/Not Sure
I recognize my emotional responses to most situations while I am experiencing them	
I handle setbacks and criticism in a constructive manner	
I adjust my emotions, thoughts and behaviour to reflect the situation	
I am aware of the impact on and impression I am creating with others	
I find it easy to read other people's emotions and adapt my behaviour accordingly	
I demonstrate emotional control when necessary	
I can understand and can name my own feelings	

The following ideas can help you to develop your capability:

- Reflect over some recent interpersonal situations and focus on how you behaved, how you felt and how you responded to the others. Describe your emotional responses to the situation. What were you feeling? Was your response constructive, appropriate and effective? How did the others react to you? Was the dialogue and process productive? The essence in this sort of reflection is to establish whether you have the ability to work in the moment with your own reactions and adapt your behaviour to ensure that the interpersonal process is effective and constructive.

- Get into the habit of self-observation and begin to assess how you react to different types of people and situations. Focus on identifying your emotional responses and triggers in various situations so that you can adapt and adjust accordingly. Awareness is half the battle.

- When you are in emotionally charged situations, ask yourself how you feel – try to describe the feeling. This will help you to understand your reactions, possible responses and, often, the triggers that can lead to overly emotional responses. Learning to understand your feelings and how they drive your behaviour can lead to better emotional control and, ultimately, more effective working relationships.

- Practice recognizing other people's emotions by being fully attentive when in dialogue with others. Maintain eye contact and look out for cues and clues in their facial expression, body language, language and style of response to help you assess their emotional state. This then helps you to plan how you will respond to ensure an effective process and outcome.

- Ask trusted others to give you feedback about your behaviour and how it affects the process of discussions. Getting used to asking for and receiving feedback is in itself demonstrating good emotional awareness. Of course, it also depends on taking notice of the feedback and adapting as necessary.

There is much written about emotional awareness, and author Dan Goleman is one of the main contributors in this area. His book *Emotional Intelligence* introduces the reader to the major theories and practices around emotional awareness and intelligence. If this is an area you feel you need to develop, then exploring some of his work will be helpful. There is also a new book by a colleague of ours, Dr Kerrie Fleming – *The Leader's Guide to Emotional Agility* – which is specifically written to help practising managers develop in this area.

- **Deals with ambiguity**

In today's complex, uncertain and ever-changing life and business environment, having the capability to deal with ambiguity in an effective way is vital when managing both your relationships and your career. Many of us talk about welcoming and enjoying change. The thing we dislike is the uncertainty and ambiguity associated with change.

Key indicators of being able to deal effectively with ambiguity are having the ability to adapt easily to change, taking on new challenges and facing risks, dealing with the unfamiliar and being able to make decisions when you only have part of the story. Dealing with ambiguity is about your reactions when faced with uncertainty and change. Do you have a 'positive let's get on with it attitude', or do you 'question everything and put up barriers until you feel completely certain?' Which is more like you?

Some personality types find dealing with ambiguity more challenging than others. If you are one of these people, who tend to like structure and order in your life, you will probably find ambiguous situations more challenging than those people who tend to be more comfortable with and excited by uncertainty and change. However, even for very structured people, it is possible to change your mindset.

As you develop in your career, and if you move into more senior positions, your experience will, of course, help you to deal with some levels of ambiguity; however, in the world today there are always new challenges presenting themselves that mean you often have to cope with new ideas, situations and circumstances: for instance, in new markets, in different cultures, in matrix organizations, changing personnel, especially if at senior levels, and that's just a few.

Reflection. Think back over the past year and identify a time when you had to deal with an ambiguous situation. Reflect about:

- your feelings and emotions while you were dealing with it
- what you actually did
- what helped/hindered the process
- anything new that you have learnt from this situation

Here are some ideas to help you understand and deal with ambiguity:

- Recognize that life today is far less certain than it appeared to be in the past. There are rarely right and wrong answers to many situations, and sometimes doing your best is not enough. It is also often impossible to wait for all the facts before making a decision.

Mistakes are allowed on occasions and can prove to be amazingly good learning opportunities.

- While planning is great, you also have to be prepared to adapt a plan to deal with new ideas and information, flexing and taking diversions when necessary. So, having backup plans and strategies is a useful way of dealing with some ambiguous situations. For instance, we often see people who are thrown by having the time available for a presentation shortened – this happens more frequently than you might think, so don't be one of those people who have to follow a planned script. Have a backup plan – maybe work from a summary note of your script so that you are able to cover the key elements and miss out some of the detail. Alternatively, have a slide with three key points that you can use if your time is shortened.

- Work with and trust others – share information to help make sense of situations and thus deal with the uncertainty and complexity together with others.

- Be curious and questioning to glean as much information as you can from people in your network, but know when the time for inquiry is over and action is required.

- **Articulate**

As a woman in business, being articulate when presenting in meetings and in any interpersonal situation will demonstrate confidence and capability. Skill in this area will also contribute to the creation and development of your reputation and credibility.

Articulacy is the art of being able to express yourself eloquently, fluently and clearly. This enables you to hold and engage with your audience, whoever that may be. Most of us are pretty articulate when talking about something we are passionate about with either our work colleagues or our friends. However, in our research, many of the respondents talked about situations when they suddenly found their ability to be articulate challenged. These included when they were over-worried about what the group would think about them or their contribution, when speaking to a group of predominantly senior men, when presenting at big events, and when they experienced people who patronized them or put them down in some way.

In our experience, articulacy comes from knowledge of your subject, thorough preparation, a passion about your subject, and practice. In addition to this, it is about your communication skills in terms of how you engage with an audience, respond to the atmosphere in the room, and use your voice and language.

There are many examples of people in the public eye who demonstrate exceptional articulacy and make it look easy, and some people are naturally gifted; however, as Mark Twain said, 'it usually takes more than three weeks to prepare a good impromptu speech'. Don't be fooled by people who make it look easy, as they have undoubtedly practised and honed their speech or contribution so that they know the points they wish to make and can do so without notes. Never try to wing it – preparation really is key.

Reflection. Certain situations are, of course, more challenging than others. Examples include getting a hearing in a meeting where there are many people with mixed views and feelings about what is being discussed, or speaking to a conference or big group. Think about the times when you feel that your articulacy is challenged. How does it make you feel? What have you done about it until now? As we have said many times before, awareness is key, and this enables you to develop some coping strategies.

The following tried and tested tips can help:

- Practise with a trusted friend or friendly audience.
- Before you start talking, take a few deep breaths to ground yourself.
- Make sure your posture is as upright as possible to give your voice a better timbre. So, if sitting, be straight, not slumped in the chair, and if possible stand up.
- If giving a formal presentation to a group, take a few seconds before you start talking to look at the group and smile. People will smile back, and this relaxes you – then start.
- If talking in a meeting, start with a link statement – for instance, 'if I can just explain my perspective ...' or 'I'd like to add a point. ...' This gives the others in the meeting a chance to get used to your voice before you make your main points.
- Always think about your opening remarks – people take very little time to decide whether or not you are worth listening to, so making an attention-grabbing early statement can be powerful.
- Make sure you know what your key points are, and try to maintain eye contact with your audience, whether one to one, in a meeting or in a

big group. Keep it short and succinct. Waffle and filler statements are completely unnecessary and distracting.

- Allow people to ask you questions, and prepare for this by anticipating what people might ask.
- Finish with something memorable.
- If someone interrupts you, talks over you or finishes your statement, then try some of the techniques used by politicians – Margaret Thatcher was good at this. Listen and thank them for their contribution, but then go on to add 'but if I could just finish what I was going to say'. Techniques like this must be used with care, as they can come across as combative or patronizing.
- If possible, go on a training course to develop your ability – not just a simple presentation skills course, though this will help, but places such as RADA (The Royal Academy of Dramatic Art) now run courses for business people using many of the techniques that are taught to actors. Look at their website: www.radainbusiness.com.
- Above all – know your topic, plan what you want to say, and practise.

When we asked our respondents for the advice they would give their younger self, many mentioned this area.

'Learn to be an assertive, articulate communicator without coming across as aggressive'

'Don't care so much about what other people think of you and always make sure that your voice is heard'

'Learn to be very good at presentations, they will act as an effective mirror of your capabilities'

Chapter 6

Essential relationship skills and qualities

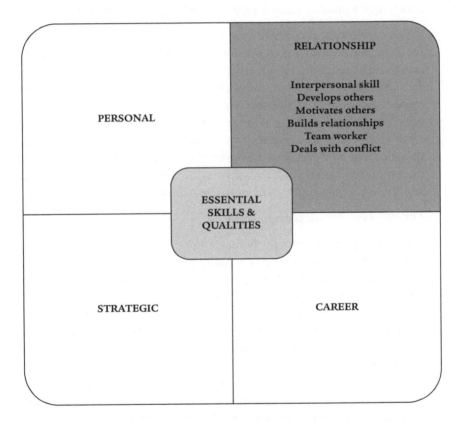

Relationship skills and qualities, often referred to as soft skills, are increasingly part of every job, career and profession and are also recognized as being vital for success. We believe there are literally no jobs where relationship skills do not add value. We have identified what we believe to be six of the main areas to focus on. Of course, this is a massive area, and the six skills and qualities we have selected are a starting point and will overlap to some degree.

- **Interpersonal skill**

  Interpersonal skill covers a broad range of different skills, all of which contribute to how we interact and communicate with other people and will contribute to your effectiveness in most of the other capabilities. In many ways, interpersonal skill is one of the bedrock skills for success in your personal and professional life, and typically, this is an area where women are often regarded as having an edge over men.

  When people talk about women's leadership styles or approaches, they tend to talk about women's ability with soft skills, which characterizes them as empathetic, sensitive and interdependent, many of which are demonstrated by their use of the key interpersonal skills. It is also important to say that twenty-first-century thinking about leadership now recognizes that these skills and capabilities are necessary for both men and women to succeed in this new era of leadership. Of course, they need to be developed and demonstrated together with some of the more traditional skills for success, but skill and capability in these key areas will give you a good springboard from which to operate.

  The most important interpersonal skills are:

  - **Listening** – involves actively focusing on what other people say and how they say it. Listening is actually part of a complex process that involves, among other things, the other four interpersonal skills. So, when you are listening, ask yourself: Are you really taking on board what the other people are saying? Are your follow-up questions linked to what they actually said? Have you picked up on clues and cues indicated by the way they expressed themselves, the nuances of how they used their voice – tone, pace, timbre, pauses? Did you notice any signals of feelings or emotions from their non-verbal communication? Are you demonstrating true social awareness by using the full range of your communication skills when listening to others?

    Your listening is also affected by how you yourself are feeling and what your own thoughts and ideas are about the subject under discussion. It is very easy to become distracted by your own thoughts and emotions when listening. So, without denying these facts, it is important to focus and maintain a positive curiosity to ensure you demonstrate your skills to the best. Also, be aware that multitasking means you are not listening effectively.

- **Smart questioning** – is about gathering information and is the basis for any successful dialogue. Good questioning also demands good listening and observation skills to ensure your questions are appropriate and relevant to the speaker and topic. For good quality dialogue and conversation, you must listen to what the person is telling you, then use appropriate questions to do one of the following:

  o To get more information
  o To test your understanding
  o To encourage further thought and exploration of the topic
  o To clarify a point
  o To control the conversation

  When asking questions, it is also important to give the other person an opportunity to answer, so use silence effectively here.

- **Non-verbal communication** is about the way a person uses their voice and body language when in interpersonal situations. Much can be gleaned from a person's vocal usage, so be aware of:

  o The pace – the speed at which a person talks: too fast and others may not keep up; too slow and people will lose interest.
  o The pitch – the variation in tone and inflection, which can be used for emphasis and demonstration of energy and enthusiasm.
  o Use of pause – people use a pause for several different reasons: to gather their thoughts, to add emphasis and to convey confidence.
  o The volume – awareness of a person's natural volume is useful; some people are naturally soft when they speak, while others tend to boom. Neither is right or wrong; it is simply important to be aware of a person's natural timbre.

  There is much written about body language. The important issue for successful interpersonal skill is to be aware of clusters of non-verbal movements and whether or not the non-verbal behaviour is synchronous with the situation and topic. So, pay attention to body movements, hand and arm gestures, eye contact, postures and facial expression. Sudden changes can indicate changes in the speaker's mood or feelings about the conversation. For instance, if you notice someone raising their eyebrows during a conversation, or if they become more mobile or agitated, this tends to indicate that something is changing for them.

- **Social awareness** is largely about demonstrating empathy when communicating with others. Empathy is having the ability to take others' perspective into account and to actively work with others, adapting and adjusting to ensure good interpersonal relationships. You can easily demonstrate empathy by:
  - Listening actively.
  - Using questions to test understanding and explore issues.
  - Paraphrasing to clarify you understand their perspective.
  - Summarizing to show others that you have listened and understood. This is especially important to make sure everyone agrees on next steps.
  - Adjusting your own perspective or views as a result of empathy.

Lack of empathy is one of the areas that many women in our survey mentioned as a barrier:

> 'My female manager has no empathy or sympathy for me and makes me feel bad for my failures too.'

In fact, it seems that some female managers and colleagues come in for quite a bit of criticism in terms of lacking empathy.

Reflection. All of the above aspects of interpersonal skill can be developed, and it is important to be honest with yourself about your skill level in any of the key components. A good way of assessing your skill in this area is to ask others for feedback. So, select a trusted colleague who sees you operate in a variety of different situations, and ask them to observe you during one such situation and give you feedback. When you ask for feedback from others, it is always best to chunk it up. So, be specific: ask for feedback on your questioning during one meeting, then perhaps ask them another time to focus on your awareness of non-verbal behaviour, and so on.

- **Develops others**

This involves taking responsibility, and having a predilection, for developing and coaching others. Whether or not you have responsibility for other people, you can still have a development focus and help both yourself and others to develop in their role and career. People who are good at this show a genuine interest in their colleagues and are constantly on the lookout for learning opportunities in the workplace.

They will often act as a mentor or coach to others, and if they are a line manager, they are aware of their team members' skills, abilities and ambitions and actively support them to develop further.

Developing others is more of an attitude than a skill per se, though you will undoubtedly have many of the interpersonal and relationship skills in your repertoire if you are regarded as good in this area. You should also be aware that commitment to developing people helps with your reputation in the organization as someone who cares about people and who helps them adapt, adjust and develop for their own success in the organization.

In addition to recognizing this as a responsibility in the day job, it is also advantageous to take on more formal development roles as, say, a coach or mentor for others in the organization. You may also find that setting up and joining action learning networks, both in and outside your organization, will help.

Reflection. When have you taken time to help others develop? Do you act as a coach, mentor or sponsor to others? Could you do more in this area? Remember to think about this in relation to your whole life, not simply your work life.

You certainly don't want to be one of these people described by our survey respondents:

'Other female bosses who do not want you to succeed'

'Bosses who feel threatened by ambitious talented women'

'Lack of support from my immediate superior'

If this is an area that interests you, you may find the recently published *Leader's Guide to Coaching and Mentoring* by Brent and Dent useful.

- **Motivates others**

It is difficult for any of us to motivate others; however, what we can all do is support others in their motivation and ensure that demotivating and destructive forces are not present or are eliminated. In today's far more self-oriented business environment, creating a motivating working atmosphere to enable people to perform effectively is hugely important. The key with motivation is knowing what it is that motivates an individual. Part of a survey we did a few years ago – The Ashridge

Management Index – identified the main motivators for managers in organizational life. The top six of these are:

- being treated with respect
- challenging/interesting work
- opportunity to continually learn and develop
- knowing my decisions have an impact on the organization
- having the authority and freedom to run my own show
- working in a pleasant environment

Interestingly, when colleagues asked Generation Y employees a similar question in their own research study, they said their top three were:

- salary
- challenging work
- career progression

So, in this area the key seems to be understanding what it is that motivates both yourself and your colleagues to allow you to contribute to providing a working environment that enables people to motivate themselves.

Reflection. Why not start these processes by reviewing what it is that motivates you? Use the space below to make a note of these. Then, select three or four of your team and list what motivates them. If you don't know, then you may have to take some time to engage with them to find out. Once you have a better understanding of these motivators, you can begin to assess your skill in this area and, if necessary, develop it further.

Key motivators for me and my team			
My motivators	Team member 1	Team member 2	Team member 3

- **Builds relationships**

  One of the main areas identified in both our survey and interviews for contributing to individual success in organizational life today was in relation to building relationships and networking both inside and outside work.

  'Building a great support network'

  'A strong internal and external network is essential for support and business intelligence'

  'I'd go and speak to people and do what nowadays is called relationship development'

  The last quote above is certainly a starting point – relationship building is all about engaging others in meaningful and genuine conversation. In this highly technological age, many people overlook the importance of face-to-face communication as a way of building relationships at work.

  In a previous piece of research for our last book, one of our interviewees talked about the importance of developing strategic relationships throughout her career. These were people whom, once she'd met them, she actively cultivated over time. Now, this may seem a little Machiavellian or manipulative, but it isn't. By being more focused and having a strategy for relationship development, you will find that you don't simply have a good network but a superb one.

  Reflection. Building strong and sustained working relationships takes effort and time – it's not simply engaging in conversation; it is so much more than that. If this is an area you feel you would like to develop further, then some of the following tips should prove useful:

  - Understand who is in your relationship network. Create a mind map to illustrate those people you currently have in your network (See example on next page).
  - Think about the quality of each of these relationships and annotate your mind map – there are many ways of doing this. For instance, categorize them by how you would define them – acquaintances, colleagues or inner circle, or simply assess on a scale of 1 to 5 in terms of how you rate the relationship. (Fiona's book *Working Relationships Pocketbook*, published by Management Pocketbooks in 2009, might also help in this area.)

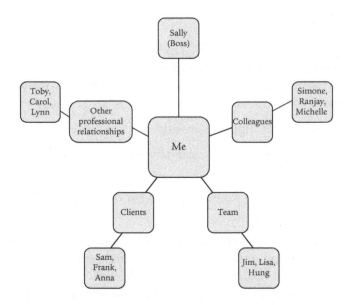

- Assess how you might better work with these people, whom you need to develop further, whether there are any people you need to add to your network, and so on.
- Identify those relationships you find most difficult and ask yourself whether there are ways to improve these.
- How would you define your relationship-building style? Are there certain types of people you get along with more than others? Is this a barrier, do you need to expand your repertoire?
- Develop a strategy for future relationship development. Identify the people or the sort of people you would like to have in your network – be purposeful about this.

Several of the interviewees we spoke to identified relationship development as an area that had helped support their career development. One woman who worked in a major international FMCG (Fast Moving Consumer Goods) organization said:

'Networking and developing good quality working relationships with colleagues has significantly contributed to my career success so far',

while another who works in a UK business organization said:

'Developing a clear plan to identify who to build networks with is definitely beneficial.'

Both these women are Generation Y and have recognized the importance and value of investing time to develop good-quality relationships at work.

- **Teamworker**

Being part of, building and leading a strong team are all elements of being a good teamworker. Not only have many women identified teamwork as a support to career success, but employers also regard this as a major contributor to organizational success. In fact, it is probably true to say that most of us work as part of at least one team. Effective teamwork can be quite a challenge, in that many of you have to deal with virtual teams, working in multiple teams, multicultural teams, short-term project teams, departmental teams, management teams and many more, some of which are not work based. This causes some challenges to effective team management, development and working, as all teams take on their own identity and demand different approaches, styles and processes. However, there are certain principles that are common to most teams, though how you apply them may be different, depending upon your role in the team and the purpose of the team.

Good teamworking demands:

- a focused, clear and involving goal
- members who are willing to work together in an interdependent way
- commitment from all team members
- a range of complementary skills and abilities
- clear rules and norms of behaviour agreed by all
- good-quality communication skills between team members
- trust and respect for each other
- understanding each other's role and contribution to the team
- support and recognition for the team and individual members
- the ability to give each other feedback

Reflection. You might like to ask yourself about the teams you are a member of and rate them on these principles. Perhaps rate each one on a scale of 1 to 5 to determine whether you or the team need to develop in any of the areas.

Lots of women who responded to our survey recognized that investment in this area was beneficial:

'Building a good team at work where trust, delegation, empowerment and focus are important'

'developing a strong team spirit and loyalty within my own team'

'Investing time and energy to develop my team and rewarding them accordingly'

Getting experience in different team environments is particularly useful, so taking opportunities to lead, build, develop and take part in teams is a great way of self and reputation development. Taking on different roles in different teams allows you to develop different skills and to test out your capabilities in multiple situations.

- **Deals with conflict**

Conflict and confrontation are facts of organizational life. Having the ability to cope with any conflict situation is a valuable asset. As one of our respondents said,

'I have had some great boss relationships, male and female bosses, but also conflict with bosses where there has been a lack of trust or respect'

We have found that many people deal with conflict badly or, alternatively, avoid it – neither strategy works well. We would like to explore how you can deal with conflict and confrontation in an effective way.

First, let's understand what conflict is. Conflict arises when there is a disagreement about ideas, approaches or ways of working, often caused by:

- misunderstanding and poor communication
- personality clashes, often where values differ
- rivalry between individuals, departments or teams
- selfishness and a lack of willingness to compromise
- poor management practices

Sometimes it can take a little while to recognize that conflict exists, and this is very much the first challenge in dealing with conflict. It is important to remember that conflict is not always a bad thing, as it can bring issues to the surface, and as long as it is dealt with efficiently, objectively and effectively, it can actually be beneficial.

The following process is adapted from *The Leader's Guide to Managing People* by Brent and Dent and suggests the six steps that will contribute to dealing with conflict effectively.

A process for dealing with conflict

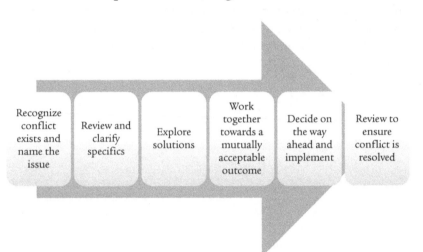

Recognize conflict exists and name the issue | Review and clarify specifics | Explore solutions | Work together towards a mutually acceptable outcome | Decide on the way ahead and implement | Review to ensure conflict is resolved

Conflict is a messy business, and while having a process to follow can help, it is also worthwhile recognizing that typically emotions play a major role in dealing with any conflict or confrontation. Being aware of both your own and others' emotional responses to the situation will enable you to plan out your process more realistically. Another key aspect of dealing with conflict is having clarity around the actual issue. Many people either forget or avoid this area. So, stage one in the process above is an essential starting point. Also, don't just launch into a conflict resolution discussion; give yourself time to think and plan. Sometimes it is necessary to allow time for people to calm down, and on occasions it can be beneficial to involve a mediator to help you navigate the process.

Dealing with conflict involves a wide range of interpersonal and relationship skills and can challenge even the most experienced and skilful people. So, choose your battles wisely and recognize that each situation is unique.

Reflection. How have you dealt with conflict in the past? Are you an avoider, an accommodator, or do you face it head on? Think about a time in the recent past when you have had to deal with a conflict. Reflect back to the situation. How did you react? What did you say, do, feel? What could you have done differently to be more effective?

If you want to explore this area in more detail, *Difficult Conversations: How to Discuss What Matters Most* by Stone, Patton and Heen of the Harvard Negotiation Project is a useful starting point.

Chapter 7

Essential strategic skills and qualities

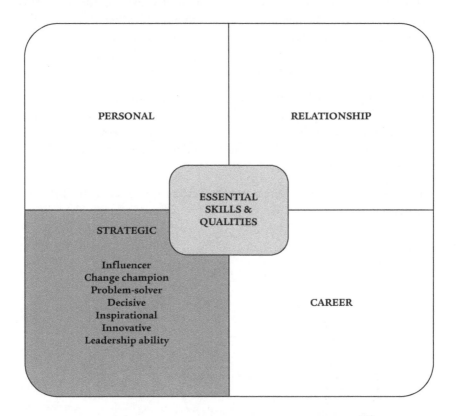

These skills and qualities are important for success as you develop and move up in an organization – they are, of course, useful at any level, but as you move into more senior positions, they become ever more necessary. The strategic capabilities may well come more easily to some personality types than others, so some people may find that some of them come naturally while others have to work hard to develop them.

Each of the skills and qualities we have selected appears in most senior management competence assessment questionnaires, so being aware of your own capability in these areas and getting a head start by developing your skill and aptitude should support your overall career development whether or not you plan to move to senior levels. They are all important capabilities for success in the volatile, uncertain and complex world we live in.

• **Influencing**

Influencing is very much a life skill. Capability and confidence in this area will certainly help you in all areas of your life. Most of us are influencing people on a day-to-day basis – in the home, at work, in shops, on the telephone, in emails – and honing your skill and understanding more about the process of influencing will be useful whatever you do.

Influencing is largely about effective use of the so-called soft skills in a strategic way. Deploying your abilities with skill and confidence, and recognizing that influencing is an interrelated process rather than a single one-off event, will help you to understand what is necessary to influence effectively.

The following diagram illustrates the key components of the influencing process:

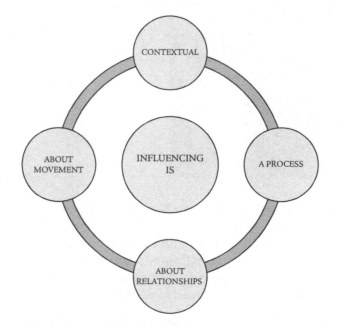

Adapted from *The Leader's Guide to Managing People*
By Mike Brent and Fiona Elsa Dent

So, during any influencing process, you must take account of:

- **The context** – every influencing situation is different. This means that the approach and style you use should be appropriate for each different context, varying and flexing your style and behaviour to suit the people and the particular situation rather than relying on one approach for all situations. This is often one of the main challenges when influencing others.
- **The process** – most influencing situations are part of a bigger process. You usually know, or at least are familiar with, most of the people you have to influence, and therefore the influencing may have already started before you meet to discuss the issue. Remember, your reputation will tend to precede the meeting.
- **The relationships** – influencing is all about getting people to buy into your ideas and work with you willingly. So, thinking about the people you have to influence and what works for them, and then varying your approach accordingly, will not only improve your influencing success but also help you to build effective working relationships.
- **Movement** – ultimately, influencing is about getting people to take steps in the direction you are proposing. It is rare that people totally agree with you at the first effort, so success as an influencer is about those small steps people take in your direction, the steps that lead to further dialogue and progression towards a mutually acceptable goal.

As we have already said, successful influencing is largely about deploying your soft skills and recognizing that influencing is a relationship skill. There are, however, certain other considerations that must be taken into account, and these are mostly about appealing to the other person's needs when engaging them in dialogue about your issue. When questioned about how individuals like to be influenced, we have found that certain themes emerge:

- **Involve them in the process**. People want to feel that their perspective on the issue is being taking account of.
- **Demonstrate confidence about the topic**. People want to feel that you genuinely know what you are talking about and that you can show energy and conviction about the topic.
- **Have a good track record of success.** Previous experience of you working well with others to reach mutual outcomes – as we said earlier, your reputation will either help or hinder you.

- **Show appreciation for others' contributions.** This helps to build good-quality relationships and likeability. Quite simply, people are more willing to listen to people they like.
- **Provide evidence to help them understand your rationale.** People like to know and understand where you are coming from, so make sure you have access to the facts and can show what the final goal is.
- **Be clear and concise.** Getting to the point without unnecessary waffle. Presenting your case in a straightforward, articulate and concise way. Keeping the attention of your audience.
- **Demonstrate passion and energy about your topic.** This shows your commitment and confidence to others. Let's face it, if you are not passionate about the topic, how can you expect others to join you?

In our work on influencing, we have found that people want three things when being influenced by others:

Involvement

Clarity

Authenticity

What they don't want is hard-sell tactics, being patronized, use of authority, being manipulated, bullying and pressure tactics.

Reflection. You might like to consider your own approach to influencing by reflecting on the following questions:

What style of influencing do I tend to use? Typically, we all tend to have a preference for one style, which, if used to the exclusion of all others, will not be helpful. Skilful influencers vary their style to suit the situation. Looking at the four styles below and their brief descriptions, which of them do you use? Rank them in order.		
Directive	An 'I'-driven style, where people assert their own views and perspectives and expect others to follow.	
Persuasive reasoning	An issue-driven style, where the main aim is to get others to buy into your ideas.	
Collaborative	A team-oriented style, where one of the main aims is to involve others in the whole process.	
Inspirational	A people-oriented style, where one of the main aims is to appeal to people's emotions and values in order to get them involved in your influencing issue.	

To understand more about your preferred style, you may like to complete 'The Influencing Style Preference Inventory', which can be purchased from the Psychometric Department at Ashridge Business School.

How do you like to be influenced? What works? What doesn't? It is worth knowing what you expect from others, as in many instances this is what others expect also.

Think about a time when you successfully influenced others – what worked and what didn't? Make notes below. This can help you to understand areas for development.

If this is an area you wish to develop, you may find *The Leader's Guide to Influence: How to Use Soft Skills to Get Hard Results* by Mike Brent and Fiona Elsa Dent to be useful.

- **Change champion**

   When asked about managing and dealing with change, most people say that they like change; what they dislike is the uncertainty that comes with change. As a change champion, it is the uncertainty that you must be aware of, and use your skills to mitigate against the very normal human responses to this – typically variations of worry, fear, anger, frustration and mistrust.

If you are a change champion, you will be called upon to use many of the personal, relationship and strategic capabilities in order to:

- prepare people to understand changes
- involve others in the change process
- set up systems and processes to facilitate change
- manage the process to ensure the changes happen while continuing business as usual
- deal with, manage and overcome resistance to change

In our research (*The Ashridge Management Index*), we have found that most respondents accept that managing change is a significant part of their job. Yet, many also feel that they are not sufficiently prepared or trained to lead the change well, and that their organization could do more to help them.

Being a change champion means that you act not only as a supporter of change but as someone who actively manages and delivers change. The key skills of a change champion involve the full range of communication skills, relationship skills and those skills necessary for dealing with resistance.

Poor communication about change and ineffective resistance management are two of the major hurdles when it comes to change in organizational life, so focusing on your communication capability, especially in relation to your influencing skill, will prove beneficial. In addition to this, having strategies for dealing with resistance will contribute to your success as a change champion. Some tips are:

- Communicate with the resisters to understand why they resist – ask questions, listen and show your understanding. Take time over this stage; many people rush through the communication phase before others have had a chance to assimilate and get used to the idea.
- Organize meetings early on in the change process to ensure people are aware of what's happening and why.
- Recognize that very often it is not the change itself that people are concerned about; rather, they are concerned about the effect on the people and their relationships – the human element – especially if it involves redundancy or other reorganization.

- Try to get resisters involved by giving them a role to play. Getting resistant people on board, especially those who are influential in their own right, can pay long-term dividends, but will take some effort.

Being an effective change champion will serve to raise your profile in any organization, but it is not a role to take on lightly; you must be happy to promote, support and implement organizational change.

Reflection. Think about some recent changes that have affected your personal or working life. Identify two different scenarios – one where you were positive and the other where things were a bit more tricky. Use the box below to reflect on the different situations and how you responded to them.

Dealing with change	
Positive change situation	Tricky change situation
Summarize the learning and insights you have taken from this reflection.	

If you want to understand more about how you can be an effective change champion, have a look at *The Change Champion's Field Guide: Strategies and Tools for Leading Change in Your Organization* by Carter and Sullivan.

- **Problem-solver**

Having a good aptitude and attitude for solving problems is something that would benefit most people in business. We experience problems on a day-to-day basis, with some problems being pretty simple to deal with and possibly having a right or wrong answer. However, increasingly, most of us have to deal with complex problems for which there is no right and wrong answer, and nor is there a precedent already set for the process or solution.

There are two main elements to becoming a good problem-solver: first, having a good process to follow, and secondly, understanding that solving problems requires both analytical and creative skills. A typical problem-solving process involves three main stages, and at each of these stages you will have to use a variety of skills.

A simple problem-solving process

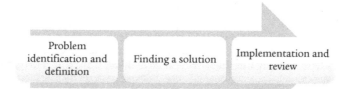

| Problem identification and definition | Finding a solution | Implementation and review |

- **Problem identification and definition.** At this stage, you will be using a range of analytical and interpersonal techniques to evaluate the situation and to gather information in relation to the problem. The key here is to be able to define and articulate the problem in your own mind and explain it to others.
- **Finding a solution.** Having defined the problem, the challenge now is to explore and consider possibilities. This could involve both analytical and creative processes – much will depend upon the problem itself. At this stage, you may also involve others to help, thus using your interpersonal, relationship and influencing skills. Your

exploration should help you to decide upon the best possible solution, based on your review and analysis.

- **Implementation and review.** Implementing your decision almost always involves others and will require you to influence people about what the solution involves and how you have reached your solution and encourage them to take it on board. Good problem-solvers also want to learn from their work and will always review how things are going, how their process worked and how people are responding to the solution.

Reflection. Think about the type of problems you have to deal with on a day-to-day basis, pick an example of one that you successfully solved and think about the key stages you went through. Which stages did you find easy/difficult, who else was involved, and were there any special techniques that you used? In this reflective process, you may also wish to consider whether or not there is a pattern to the problems you have to deal with.

Many problems cannot be dealt with in a neat linear process; you will often have to use an iterative process, going back to earlier stages during the overall process. You might find some additional helpful ideas in *The Problem Solving Pocketbook* by Ceserani and Hailstone.

- **Decisive**

Being decisive and making good decisions, not only about your career but also in relation to your job role, will serve you well. Being decisive is particularly important for those people in leadership roles, but any person working in any organization can benefit from demonstrating decisiveness in his or her day-to-day work.

We make decisions all the time: some decisions we make unconsciously, and others we agonize over. Often the ones we agonize over are those tough decisions in which we have little prior experience of the situation, or perhaps when our decision affects others. Some women tell us they have a particular problem in this area, in that when a decision adversely affects others they want to be sure that they are making the best possible decision and that they can justify it to everyone. Sometimes you have to make unpopular decisions, and the best you can hope for is that you do your homework and understand the situation, making the decision, applying the decision and reviewing your decision to ensure it is having the desired effect. Some people find it useful to use various decision-making aids such as Strengths, Weaknesses, Opportunities and Threats (SWOT) analysis, Force Field Analysis, Political, Economic, Social and Technological (PEST) analysis or brainstorming to help them with decisions. For more information on these techniques, look at www.mindtools.com.

You will sometimes be called upon to make quick decisions, often involving complex and uncertain issues. Under these circumstances, it is important that, if appropriate and time allows, you seek input from others who may be able to help, analyse the data you have, create options, and on occasions be willing to take a calculated risk if required. Don't be pushed into making a bad decision by others.

Decision-making, like many other business skills, is not an exact science, so being decisive and making well thought through decisions that impact on your own and others' performance will help build your credibility and reputation.

Reflection – You might find it useful to reflect about some of the recent decisions you have had to make. Think about:

- the process you went through to make the decision
- do you rely on data or emotions to make decisions? or perhaps both
- how successful has your decision-making been in the past?
- getting feedback from others – maybe ask whether they see you as a decision-maker or a ditherer

The Decision-Making Pocketbook by Russell-Jones and Hailstone is a valuable resource to give you additional ideas and information.

- **Inspirational**

In the Merriam-Webster online dictionary, inspiration is defined as 'something that makes someone want to do something or that gives someone an idea about what to do or create: a force or influence that inspires someone'.

To be inspirational, you must first inspire yourself, so what is it that inspires you? Some of the things that people said inspire them include:

- working for or with someone inspirational
- experiencing an inspirational teacher
- parents or other family members

- listening to an inspirational speaker
- reading an inspirational book or story
- being out in nature, taking a long walk
- listening to music
- a particular smell or sight

Reflection. So, what is it that inspires you? Seems like a simple question, but it is often quite a difficult one to answer. Take some time to think about it and reflect about what has inspired you throughout your life, and why. Make notes in the box below.

WHAT INSPIRES ME?

Now that you know what inspires you, it will be easier to think about how you can be inspirational to others. Of course, different things inspire everyone, so being inspirational to others can be a completely accidental affair. However, inspirational people do seem to share some common traits:

- **being genuine** – being value driven and authentic in all you do
- **being a positive thinker** – focusing on the positive in any given situation

- **taking an interest in others** – being available to encourage, help and support others
- **demonstrating energy and enthusiasm** – showing your own passion for the things you value
- **being willing to take the time to talk to** and inspire others

Being inspirational is often serendipitous, and many people who inspire others are surprised that they do. Adopting these five traits will help you to demonstrate an inspirational way of working and stimulate others as well.

Looking back at your reflections on how you have been inspired, think about the people who have had an effect on you. Have you ever told them they inspired you? If not, why not tell them – they may be surprised to hear it!

As a working woman, you may find inspiration in *Women Who Changed the World: Fifty Inspirational Women Who Shaped History* by Smith Davies Publishing. You might also find it useful to look at some of the presentations on TED Talks.

- **Innovative**

Being innovative does not necessarily mean that you have to come up with the next life-changing idea for the world. What it does mean is that you come up with new ideas on how things can be done and, more importantly, that you are willing to give them a try.

We live in a remarkably innovative era; for instance, who would have imagined fifty years ago that we would be able to talk to our relatives in other continents face-to-face at the push of a button (Skype), or to harness the energy of the sun for household use (solar panels), or that our telephone would be mobile, a computer, a camera, a music player, a central heating controller, and so on (the mobile phone). Many of these innovative ideas are attributed to small groups of people, and yes, people like Steve Jobs are hugely innovative, but they need others who are also innovative to work with them to bring their ideas to fruition, so being innovative is something we all have the capacity for.

In many working environments, innovation is a key contributor to future success and growth, so it is not surprising that employers today seek innovative people. Coming up with a new procedure, process or service will contribute to innovation in your workplace.

The key characteristics of innovative people are:

- **Curiosity** – a person who takes an interest in everything around them, questioning and investigating how things work and why things are the way they are.
- **Adaptability** – flexible in the way they work, with a willingness to try out new ideas.
- **Creativity** – adopts imaginative ways of doing things, often challenging the status quo.
- **Risk-Taking** – willing to experiment, move outside of their own comfort zone, and can cope with mistakes and failure if necessary.
- **Learning Orientation** – demonstrating a genuine interest in seeking out new ideas and knowledge and then integrating these into their day-to-day work.

So, **reflect** back – what have you innovated in your work/life over the past few years? How might you demonstrate your innovativeness to even better effect? Use the space below to make notes.

My innovations.

- **Leadership ability**

Having leadership ability, or perhaps we should say having a leadership mindset, is something many employers seek in their staff. In essence, this means that you demonstrate a willingness to take on responsibility for influencing, motivating and working with others in the service of goal achievement and success.

Many of the skills we have already reviewed contribute towards your leadership ability, especially those related to working with others and those discussed earlier in this chapter.

Leadership means different things to different people, and for many of us, it doesn't mean getting to the top of the organization. Rather, it means being able to lead others in some situations some of the time. Demonstrating your willingness to take on leadership positions will give you a greater choice of job role and help build your credibility and reputation.

For instance, one of our interviewees told us about a time when she attended an assessment centre for recruitment into a major retail organization. As happens in many of these assessments, part of the process involved a team exercise in which the group had to work together to meet a goal. Once the team were briefed, they started by agreeing that they needed a leader – everyone went quiet. After a few minutes of this, our interviewee thought 'Why don't I give this a go?' She got the job, and likes to think that stepping up in this exercise contributed to her success.

Reflection. When have you taken the lead in the past? It could be at work or in some other part of your life. Think about this and note down what you led, what went well and what you feel you could have done better. Being aware of the skills you use when leading and what works and what doesn't will help you to further develop as a leader.

If you have never had an opportunity to take the lead, or maybe even choose to avoid leadership roles, you might find it useful to reflect about why.

Use the space that follows to make notes:

My leadership experience/s.

One of the main things any good leader is able to do is to flex their style to suit different situations and people. This, in turn, means that you must know your people, be aware of the situation you are in and have the foresight to adapt accordingly.

Understanding your own style and preference as a leader will help you to recognize where you may need to develop further to be able to flex more easily. We heard some stories that suggested that some women conform to stereotypes when it comes to leadership style – either being more macho or conforming to the prevailing organizational style. On the whole this does not work, as you need to find your own style and be authentic.

There are many different theories about leadership style. In an earlier survey undertaken during 2011 and reported in our previous book – *Women in Business: Navigating Career Success* – we identified seven different styles. We asked women to identify what they believed to be their primary leadership style.

Reflection. You may like to do the same by ranking the following seven styles in order of YOUR preference:

STYLE	DESCRIPTOR	RANK
Participative	You actively involve others in discussion and decision-making	
Situational	You vary your style to suit the situation	
Visionary	You inspire others through your energy and commitment	
Transactional	You give direction and expect it to be met	
Value Based	You lead based on strong personal values	
Intuitive	You use a more instinctive approach in which both people and situation are considered, often described as gut feel	
Hierarchical	You rely on your position and status	

Adapted from Leadership Style in *Women in Business: Navigating Career Success* (2012) by Viki Holton and Fiona Elsa Dent.

Understanding your preference in style is important, but as many women have told us in both the previous and current research, many of them use a combination of styles. If, like us, you believe that leadership is a social skill whereby leaders must be enablers of people, then good people leadership is about your ability to adapt your approach to the people and the situation.

If you want to explore the above styles in more detail, a longer questionnaire with full explanations about each style is in our book mentioned above. There are literally thousands of books about leadership that can offer you support in this area. Much will depend upon your particular interest: some of you may wish to focus on skill development, so reading something like *The Leadership Skills Handbook* by Jo Owen will be helpful, while others may be more interested in personal leadership stories, so Sheryl Sandberg's book *Lean In* or Karren Brady's *Strong Woman* would be more beneficial.

Chapter 8

Essential career skills and qualities

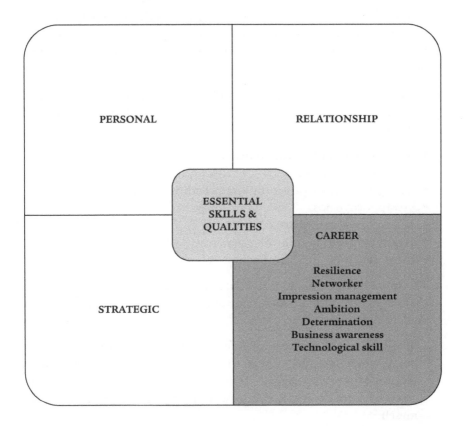

We have named the following seven areas of career skills and qualities. We believe that you should be aware of these as enablers to help you navigate the uncertain and complex world of work that we all live in today. These areas are important throughout your working life, and unlike some of the other skills and qualities, they are relevant to most of us.

- **Resilience**

Resilience is often described as being able to bounce back from adverse events and difficult situations. We see it as slightly more than this – it's about being able to deal with the day-to-day pressures that work and life throw up. It's about coping with all manner of stressful situations in a way that enables you to continue to thrive in life and work.

This does not mean that you do not experience the wide range of emotions that are so often felt when experiencing adversity. It does mean that you have developed coping strategies and can move forward in a positive way.

Many of the barriers and hurdles working women face could be termed adverse or difficult – some of the more common ones mentioned include:

- promotion opportunities blocked
- male-dominated cultures
- having to sacrifice career for family commitments
- unsupportive boss
- sexism in the workplace
- regaining position following maternity leave
- redundancy

The stories we heard about in relation to how women deal with these challenges demonstrate that many of you have resilience by the bucket load. For instance:

'Redundancy on 3 occasions. I fought and won an employment tribunal when I was 26. … I can't accept not having work and always register with a temp agency – I will take any work I can to keep myself working. I am determined, hardworking and take responsibility for myself.'

'Many barriers experienced over the years, including setbacks through high paced restructures within the organization and loss of career pathway and total role change. It's about showing how adaptable you are, resilience to circumstance and determination to succeed – the opportunity to learn and grow new skills was an advantage amongst some very trying years.'

'"My dear girl" is still a relatively common way for a male counterpart to attempt to undermine my authority in a document negotiation situation. I've overcome that by simply making sure I am technically more proficient and ensuring that comes across so that others can see the belittling tactics for what they are – much easier now I am more senior but it was hard at a junior level'

Reflection. So, how resilient are you? How do you overcome adversity? It is worth being aware of your own coping strategies and how you have overcome difficulties in the past. We all develop different ways to overcome adversity. There is no magic bullet; however, based on some of the stories we heard from the women we interviewed and those who took part in our survey, some of the following characteristics seem to help:

- thinking positively and being optimistic
- having belief in yourself
- being learning oriented
- investing in your own personal well-being
- having the ability to name and control your emotions
- recognizing when you are experiencing stress and work overload
- being solution focused
- having a strong support network

If you would like to find out more about resilience, you might find it useful to read *Resilience: How to Cope When Everything around You Keeps Changing* by Liggy Webb. If you would like to understand more about your own resilience, then you may find it useful to complete 'The Ashridge Resilience Questionnaire', available from Ashridge Business School Psychometrics Department.

- **Networker**

Building a good network was highlighted by many of the women in both our interviews and the survey as an enabler. Calling on people in their network at various stages in their career has been useful in a variety of different ways. Here's what some women said:

'building a great support network who have consistently shown faith in my abilities, guiding me and pushing me out of my comfort zone'

'One of the reasons I didn't get promoted as quickly as I would have wished was because I hadn't taken the time to effectively network and build vital relationships with key decision makers. I didn't truly understand the importance of this until I'd established a mentor relationship with a successful woman, who brought this requirement to life for me'

'I have overcome barriers through the passage of time, reaching out to friends and colleagues for support when needed, always persevering and trying to maintain a supportive network at home through family and friends'

The term *networking* has become incredibly popular in recent years with the advent of the myriad of social networking sites on the World Wide Web, and undoubtedly these can be beneficial to raise your profile and keep in touch with people. Sites such as LinkedIn, other smaller networking sites for particular professions and, of course, Facebook can be useful.

Building a network that will help you not only manage and develop your career but also get things done on a day-to-day basis involves much more than simply having a presence on the social networking sites. It's about investing time, energy and thought into building strategic relationships with various people over time.

These relationships should be mutually beneficial and based on alliances around common goals in order to be successful. Building a successful network to help you as a working woman, whether that be about building your career or managing your day-to-day work or even to support you in your work–life balance, involves authenticity, reciprocity and likeability.

Authenticity is meant in the sense that you aim to build trusting and mutually beneficial relationships through being consistent, following through on any promises, delivering what you say you will and demonstrating positive, solution-focused behaviours. Reciprocity means you are investing your time to engage with others to share information, offer support and work in collaboration to achieve results on common goals. Using these positive reciprocal behaviours when building networks and relationships will mean that others are more likely to be positively predisposed towards you and thus feel a sense of obligation towards you. Likeability in that we all tend to prefer to work and build relationships with people we like and will be inclined to help them when and if required.

Reflection. Let's face it, you simply do **not** have time to develop strong and effective networks. So, what can you do if this is something that doesn't come easily to you?

- First of all, think about who is already in your network. What role do they play? How would you rate the relationship? Is it a strong relationship built on mutuality, or is it a relationship that you feel requires more work? We find it useful to represent this in a mind map – see Question 3 'Who Supports Me' in Chapter 1 for a fuller explanation of reviewing your network.
- When you first meet people, try to find something you have in common – for instance, it could be your role, an interest, a person who connects you. This makes it easier to begin to build and develop rapport.
- Ask questions and listen – in fact, develop a range of opener questions that can be used in a variety of situations, and especially when you are in the early stages of developing a relationship.
- Think strategically about your network, be long term – you need people both in your own organization and externally with other professionals, clients, suppliers, etc. You need people in your work life and in your personal life, and they should be as diverse as possible.
- Keep in touch with your network. Don't over-saturate people with contact or information; make sure it's both timely and relevant. You never know when you will need your network, so maintaining the various relationships is time well spent. Why not try inviting them to any relevant events, sharing something with them you know they might find useful and interesting – articles, books, research, and so on? If you happen to be in their area, drop in to see them. Just a quick hello is all that's necessary, or arrange to meet for coffee or lunch: whatever is appropriate for you both.
- Think about what you can do for the people in your network; remember that good-quality strategic networks are built on mutuality and reciprocity. If you get the previous point right and keep in touch around things you believe will be helpful to the individuals, this is one way of showing others that you are genuine and authentic.

Remember – networking is about building good-quality long-term relationships in which you can support and help each other. It's really all about sincerity and caring about other people, not about giving out business cards and meeting as many people as possible.

These words from Maya Angelou probably summarize better than we can what networking is really all about:

> 'I've learned that people will forget what you said, people will forget what you did, but people will never forget how you made them feel.'

• Impression management

Impression management is about self-presentation. It's the manner in which you portray yourself to others, the impact you have on others and the image you are trying to create. It affects how you influence others, how you create credibility and build your reputation. Do not underestimate the power of creating a good impression.

Erving Goffman wrote about impression management in his seminal work *The Presentation of Self in Everyday Life*, published in 1959. He believed that when people come into contact with one another, each individual will attempt to guide or manage the impressions the other might form of them. In more recent years, the concept of impression management has become widely recognized as a vital element of our relationship-building skills. Successful individuals realize that building and creating positive lasting impressions will contribute to their effectiveness, their personal credibility and their reputation.

It's important to remember that when people meet you (face-to-face, during a meeting, at a presentation or at a social event, to name but a few possibilities), whether consciously or subconsciously, they are asking themselves a range of questions:

- What do I think about this person?
- Do I like this person?
- Could I work with this person?
- Do I trust what this person is saying and doing?
- Could I respect this person?
- Do I want this person in my relationship network?

The answers to these questions will then contribute to how your relationship with the person will progress. But, more than that, they will also have an effect on how that person might represent you to others. In our increasingly connected world, how you present yourself, not only in face-to-face interactions but also when using technology – emails, conference calls, when tweeting or blogging, on social media, and so on – has an effect on the impression you are creating. In recent years, there have been many instances of the media reporting on an individual's inadvertent inappropriate tweet, or other social media comment, that has then impacted on their reputation, and not often in a good way!

So, as working women, this is certainly an area we must all be very aware of. In our research, we heard lots of evidence of women who recognized this, and many women who have recognized it later in their career and wished they had done so earlier.

> 'This is a tricky one. I love fashion and because I have been well paid I have tended to eschew suits for designer clothing – nothing terribly outlandish but garments that are more colourful and more alternative than most people would wear who work in the public sector in a management position. Looking back I do think I have been judged for it. Although it pains me to say this, because I am a big believer in people being able to express themselves creatively through their clothes I would probably say to my younger self to tone the clothes down slightly for work!'

> 'Be conscious of how you come across to other people. Walk the walk of the person doing the next job up.'

> 'You really need to demonstrate in your manner and work that you are "on board" or "back on board" after having had a baby to not lose ground'

The model below summarizes the major components of impression management:

Impression management

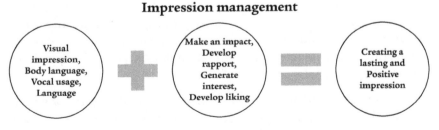

Adapted from: Dent and Brent *The Leader's Guide to Managing People*

Reflection. It's important to take time to think about the image, impression and impact you will be having on others each and every time you interact with them, no matter which communication method you are using. Think about:

- Your appearance – is it appropriate for the situation and context? If in doubt, go formal and smart rather than informal and too casual.
- What you say and how you say it.
- The situation and people you will be interacting with.
- Focus on being consistent – remember you are building your reputation, so consistency is important.
- Demonstrate authenticity – people have natural antennae that pick up inauthenticity, and there is nothing more off-putting than trying to manipulate who you are.
- Be yourself, and be aware of the impact you have on others. Don't try to act; most of us can't keep an act up for long.
- What you want people to feel about you when you leave them.
- Remember – it can take years to build a good reputation, yet it can be destroyed in seconds! As one of our respondents put it,

'Remember what goes around comes around, so be considerate in all your dealings with others. (It took me a long time to learn this).'

You may find Judith Humphrey's book *Taking the Stage: How Women Can Speak Up, Stand Out and Succeed* an interesting read.

- **Ambition**

Ambition is about your desire to achieve. Having ambition at work is a good thing, and without it you will find that you can wander aimlessly from job to job. It is about having aspirations and goals to aim for. Ambition is not necessarily about getting to the top. Ambitious people don't always want to be the best at something or get to the top; what they want is to fulfil their own aspirations, goals and dreams. Women sometimes hesitate to talk about their ambitions, but if people don't know they can't help you.

In a research study on a sample of 2,960 men and women, of whom 49 per cent were men and 51 per cent women, undertaken in 2011 by the Institute of Leadership and Management (*Ambition and Gender at Work*), they found that women tended to set their sights lower than men do and settle for less. They also found in their survey that 52 per cent of the male managers had a fair idea or clear ambition to work in a particular role, while this applied to only 45 per cent of the women surveyed.

We also found evidence in our study that many women played down their ambitions, mainly due to lack of self-confidence or self-belief (see earlier). There are also the obvious barriers or hurdles that have an effect upon a woman's ambitions, including taking maternity leave, being a working mother, being part of a dual-career couple and working in male-dominated environments. We accept that these all exist, and they are all surmountable. You may have to put some ambitions on hold for a while, or find ways of getting round the hurdles, but having ambitions and demonstrating ambition will help with your career success.

Again, we found that many women offered their advice to their younger self in relation to this area.

'Understand that if there is something you want to achieve in life, business or personally it's down to you! No-one will do it for you.'

'I have always recognized that women hold back and wait until they feel "ready" when in reality, sometimes the only way to be "ready" is to apply for the job, and if successful, apply yourself to the job.'

'Leave the nice, safe, comfy job and go for the one that scares you.'

There were lots of similar quotes, often indicating that while ambitious, many allowed their lack of self-confidence to get in the way or were negatively affected at some stage in their early career, which led to them playing down their ambitions.

Reflection. What are your ambitions? Make a note of them NOW. What do you want to achieve in the next year, five years, ten years ...? Think one job ahead. Use the box below to make a note – be concise, focused and specific. For instance: apply for an international posting this year, get promoted in the next year, leave to find a better job, or run a half marathon in the next six months.

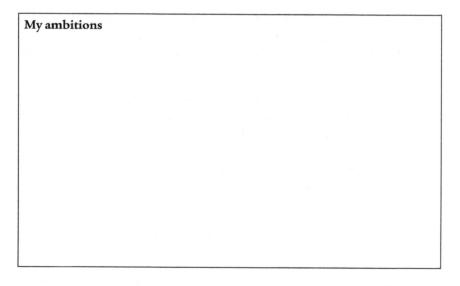

My ambitions

- **Determination**

This is another attribute that many employers seek today; it is also one that many of you mention as something that has helped you get to where you are today. Many believe that without a combination of determination, resilience and ambition they would not have progressed to the positions they are in today.

'I overcame the barriers put in my way by determination and hard work'

'Determination not to give up no matter how tough things got; asking even if the answer was "no" and keeping going, holding my nerve.'

'The only way to overcome barriers is through sheer self determination and deliver over and above your goals'

Being determined is all about focus and commitment to achieving a goal. So, as your starting point, you must have a worthwhile goal. Having the goal gives you something to aim for. Of course, the goal must be simple, clear, realistic, attainable and personal to you. You may have to take diversions along the way to overcome obstacles and hurdles, but having that goal keeps you focused. If it is a worthwhile goal, then you will stick with it and work hard to achieve it. Sometimes people set themselves ridiculously ambitious goals and targets, and when they fail to achieve them, they feel deflated. However, setting staged goals so that you achieve one level and then move on to the next is often more practical.

It is very easy to give up on something because it seems to be too difficult, and this is why we say it is important to have a worthwhile and well thought through goal. People who show determination will tend also to demonstrate:

- self-confidence
- self-belief
- ambition
- resilience

Reflection. Thinking back through your life, are there any areas where you regret not following through and pursuing a goal? What was it that stopped you? Now, think about a time when you have achieved your goal. What was it that drove you during this time? What are your current goals? Now and for the future?

If you want to get some inspiration about determination, then you may find the following two books interesting: *I Am Malala: The Girl Who Stood Up for Education and Was Shot by the Taliban* (2014) by Malala Yousafzai and Christina Lamb, and *Bounce: How Champions Are Made* (2010) by Matthew Syed.

- **Business awareness**

Understanding the big picture of business, whether that be in general or more specifically for your particular sector or firm, is an area that many employers are increasingly expecting from their staff. Certainly, a good grasp of business in general will contribute to your overall career success.

One simple way of building knowledge in this area is reading the business pages in any of the national newspapers, or regularly reading the *Financial Times* or journals such as the *Economist*. Membership of the professional body associated with your chosen career or joining local business groups such as Chambers of Commerce will also help in this area, as well as providing you with good networking opportunities.

By business awareness, we mean having a good appreciation of the general business environment that exists today: including, for instance, understanding your sector, who your competitors are, where opportunities lie, and how these might be affected by external factors such as the prevailing political and economic environment.

Reflection. So, you might like to think about how much you know already, especially in relation to your own business or business sector. A useful starting point is to do a SWOT analysis of your own business/organization. Use the chart below to begin your analysis. When you are completing this chart, think about both internal and external factors, take account of competitors and how they operate, and consider the general economic and political environment for your sector.

My business awareness SWOT

My Business's/Organization's Strengths	My Business's/Organization's Weaknesses
Opportunities for my Business/Organization	Threats to my Business/Organization

If you want to develop your skill and knowledge in this area, then you may find that attending an MBA or enrolling on a short programme at a Business School would be helpful. However, that would not be enough – you need to keep up to date as well. As we suggested earlier, reading a good-quality newspaper and your professional journal will go a long way towards helping you.

- **Technological skill**

  Staying on top of technology and continuously building your own confidence, knowledge and proficiency is vital in our technological age. Success in any workplace demands that you have a good understanding of the day-to-day technology that can help with your performance and effectiveness. So, whatever your line of work, technology will play a part. As writers, we have to have a good understanding of the capabilities of Microsoft Word so that we can work with the layout and presentation of our book, not to mention how to use the various functions that help with spelling, punctuation, cutting and pasting, and so on. ... And that's not the only technology that we use – Skype comes in handy for research interviews, and there are online survey tools, social media for promoting our research, and, of course, the multitude of 'Apps' that have been developed.

  It is also interesting to note that many successful organizations have fallen by the wayside or lost their way for a while by not keeping up to date or not recognizing that things were changing. Examples include Kodak, which missed opportunities in the digital photography area, and Nokia, which at one point was the market leader in mobile phone production, but was overtaken by Apple and the various Androids that developed the smart phone. We are sure you can think of your own examples of other organizations that have suffered by not recognizing the impact of the fast movement of technology on their business.

  At a personal level, we are not suggesting that you all become super whizz kids with programming or coding (though we gather these skills are now being taught in the classroom, so watch out, as the next generation of technologically savvy young people will certainly be much more competent with technology than any other generation). What we are suggesting is that you become skilful in using the tools that can help you be successful and efficient and stay up to date in your job, career and life.

  Reflection. Use the quiz below to assess your proficiency in some of the most popular technological aids to work and life today. Think about how aware you are of what the aid can do for you, what your skill is in using it, and whether or not you need to develop greater proficiency. The simplest way of doing this is to score yourself on a scale of 1 to 5, where 1 means having little awareness or skill and 5 being a bit of an expert. Then decide whether it is an area you need to develop by indicating yes or no.

For those of you who are very technologically aware, we have no doubt missed out some common or useful aids. We accept that this shows our own lack of awareness in this area, but what we hope is that it will make many of you recognize that technology is here for keeps, it is always changing and improving, and all of us have to learn to work with it and use it to make us more effective and efficient. Even the most technologically savvy recognize that they must stay current and keep developing. This area really is an ongoing process for everyone. In this list, we have included both gadgets/devices and services.

Technology quiz

Technological aid	Awareness of the versatility and uses	My skill level	A development area for me?
Personal computer (or laptop) and its software			
iPad or tablet			
Mobile phone			
Smart phone			
Skype			
Twitter			
Blogging			
Using other social media, for example, LinkedIn, Facebook			
Video conferencing			
Software packages, for example, for Word documents, spreadsheets, presentations			
Apps you have downloaded			
Others			

As baby boomers, we have found over the years that we have had to become proficient ourselves in using technology, and in our experience the following tips have helped us:

- Get on a course to give you the basics.
- Use the tools – don't delegate this, at least until you have gained a good understanding of what's possible with the technology you need to do your job. So, for instance, if you work in research or finance, it is helpful to understand the range of possibilities of using spreadsheet software. This means that, while you don't have to do all the coding and inputting yourself, you will understand the versatility of the package and what's possible and what's not. Practice really does work where technology is concerned.
- Be curious, talk to tech-savvy people to find out about what's new and ask them questions to ascertain whether something new is going to help you. It is always best to identify the tech-savvy person who is willing and able to explain in layman's language!
- Be aware of both the gadgets (mobile phones, tablets, watches, etc.) and the various services (cloud technology, voice over internet protocol (VOIP)) that are available to help you.

Finally,

In Chapters 4–8, we have reviewed twenty-nine skills and qualities that many employers seek and, we believe, contribute to success at work. We hope that these short discussions about each of them will help you to review your skill and will give you ideas for further development in any that you have selected to focus on.

Chapter 9

Making it happen!

Go for it! That's our conclusion and what we think many women need to do with their career. Take control of your career, get more structured, set out a plan and make it happen! And don't forget to re-arrange your plan as necessary. Don't let your career simply drift along. Take hold of opportunities when they come your way, and remember to create your own opportunities: look for chances to be a volunteer for key projects where you are working, look around you all the time, be curious to meet new people and learn about what they do in the company. Comments from our respondents include:

'when you take on a new job accept every invitation you get!'

One woman felt that, while she could see her reputation in the company was reasonable, she needed something 'extra' if she was going to make an impression for the senior role she wanted. Over the next few years, she took on external voluntary roles – one at a professional organization and another with a key sector organization. She organized workshops and study tours and spoke at conferences – all areas that gave her valuable experience, and she built a good reputation outside the company. She would find that she was often asked to be a speaker or to get involved with different initiatives. These external roles gradually made a difference to the way her colleagues within the company regarded her.

So far in this book, we have encouraged you to review your career to date by undertaking a career audit and thinking about where you are now. We have also shared with you what women in our interviews and surveys say, and suggested a range of skills and qualities that we believe contribute to any individual's career success. The challenge now is to begin to think about how you can action what you have learnt about yourself and your working life to make sure you have a career future that works for you.

Some people find that their careers go amazingly well, but for others it can be a very rocky road. It's important to bear this in mind, as otherwise you'll be put off by the first barrier or if you get 'stuck' in a job that you hate or with a boss whom you don't like. Similarly, too much concern about what others will think about you can paralyse you – will people think I'm too pushy? Is it OK to say I'm ambitious?

So, don't step back, step forward. Don't be shy about asking for help, as in our experience most people are flattered to be asked for their advice, and many of us, most of us, would willingly reach out a hand to help a colleague, a friend or someone who needs our help. Also, take time to reflect and learn about what happens to you at work. You will make mistakes along the way, but making a mistake is not a crime; it is only a crime if you don't learn from it and instead simply rush headlong into a similar mistake.

You are the key player in planning and managing your career; however, it is important to understand that both circumstances and luck also play a role. For instance, it is impossible to plan for redundancy, illness or many of the other life-changing circumstances – good or bad – that can affect our working lives.

As an example, we were recently talking to a woman who has experienced a life-changing experience that has affected her chosen career. She was a jewellery maker by trade and had to give this up due to severe rheumatoid arthritis, which affected her ability to manipulate the metals with her hands. This had a major effect on her both emotionally and psychologically, yet as she told us, 'there was a big wall in front of me which I could have crashed into but I decided to walk round it'. What she did was change medium; she is now working with wire, paint and words to create her own art. She also teaches jewellery making, thus continuing to use her knowledge but in a different way. The chronic illness still affects her physically, but she has not let it stop her following her chosen profession as an artist.

The more you know about yourself, your needs, your dreams and your desires, the better prepared you will be to deal with any change, whether it is planned or not.

As many of the women in our survey suggest,

> 'Understand that if there is something you want to achieve in life, business or personally it is down to you! No one will do it for you.'

'Target where you want to go and go for it – don't be shy and underestimate your abilities, but manage your destiny in a more structured way. (Don't lose focus).'

Influences on women managing their career

Before we look at how you can be more structured about managing your career and making things happen, let's first look at two specific areas that can have an effect on the way a woman manages her career. These are both areas that have been mentioned by our survey respondents and interviewees as influences to be aware of.

- **Stepping up** – this is an important concept that affects many women when managing their career. What we mean here is actually putting yourself forward for a new role – stepping up and moving from the familiar to something new. We heard from so many of you that you have on occasions held yourself back because you were not sure you had all the qualifications or the right experience to go for either a promotion or a new role. Largely, this is caused by what seems to be one of the biggest career barriers for women: a lack of self-belief and confidence. You told us stories of self-doubt. The three quotes below are just a small sample of the sort of things many women express.

  'My own belief in my ability to contribute at a senior level and a conservatism about applying for senior jobs. Overcome by applying for a senior job and getting it!'

  'I have been the biggest barrier to my career – doubting my own achievements and always questioning if I am good enough.'

  'I have generally worked for very good bosses throughout my career (men and women) and have been encouraged to develop. A key barrier has been the limit I put on myself, in my own abilities and that I have the knowledge and skills to do the job. Having two masters degrees is perhaps a way of convincing myself that I am legit as well as now being ultra vigilant of the self doubt voice, not that it goes away but that the volume is quietened.'

Other common issues mentioned that stop women stepping up include:

- the imposter syndrome
- working mother guilt
- no senior female role models
- wanting a good work–life balance
- male-dominated environments
- external factors – family expectations
- lack of career advice from my company

Stepping up and the timing of when you do this are, of course, your own choice. There will be times when you decide, for very good reasons, not to step up to the next role or opportunity; the important point we want to put to you is that you should not allow the above issues to get in your way.

- **Staying with or moving from an organization.** Another of the issues that women talk about is the decision to stay within or move from an organization. Many of you said you had stayed 'too long' in one role or in one organization. This is always a difficult decision to make, and is often compounded if, for instance, you are a working mother with good childcare arrangements in a local area or part of a dual-career couple so that you are limited to working within a certain radius from your home. There are many other reasons why a person chooses to stay in an organization. Again, it is about awareness; the point is to have a good reason – not simply inertia.

It's OK to stay with a company, or in a job, for a long time. A number of survey respondents asked this question, and we think if you are happy, and the job is rewarding and fulfilling, then that's great. The important test is whether you are being recognized and rewarded appropriately, or are you regarded as just a safe pair of hands who will do an efficient job while your boss takes all the glory? If you stay for a long time at one company, there are advantages – such as the fact that you know so many people and you know how to get things to happen. Some women also told us that they chose to stay in a job or an organization for convenience and flexibility, especially during early child-rearing years. The familiarity often afforded them a degree of freedom that they might not have had if they had moved to a new role or a new organization.

This is a clear choice that some working mothers (and fathers) make to ensure a good-quality work–life balance and stability for their children. Making conscious decisions is what this book is all about. By doing this, you can focus on getting the best out of your job and your life as a working woman.

But also be aware that one disadvantage for women is that people may remember that before you were marketing director, you worked in a far more junior role as an assistant. However, if you move to a new company as a marketing director, then you are simply that – the new marketing director. You might argue that this would be the same for a man, and that's true, but this earlier, more junior role history seems in our experience to have a greater negative impact on a woman's career. If you want to test out this theory in your own company, think about women at a senior level who have stayed, and then compare them with those women who have joined in the past few years from other companies.

Reflection. You may find it interesting to refer back to some of the exercises in the Career Audit chapter, especially the Personal CV and Life Timeline, and reflect about your pattern of movement in various jobs and organizations. Understanding your journey, the decisions you have made, the rationale for these decisions and the ease or difficulty you have had so far will help you in the future.

Getting help

Helping yourself by knowing yourself is one way of ensuring you thrive and survive in today's ever-changing and complex world of work. However, there are also other sources of assistance that you can draw upon, but, like everything else in this book, we suggest that you must be organized and strategic in the way you use these resources. In the chart below, we illustrate some of the key sources of help mentioned by many of you.

Reflection. At this stage, it is worth thinking through what your sources of help are, how useful they are and how frequently you access them.

Sources of Help

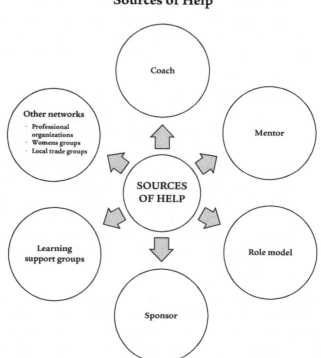

Let's look at each of these sources of help and review what their role might be in helping and supporting you.

- **A coach** – in recent years, coaching has become an incredibly popular method for supporting anyone's personal development. The main benefit is that a coach will focus purely on helping you to work through your development agenda. There are many different types of coach, including executive coaches, leadership coaches, business coaches and life coaches. No matter what tag the coach gives himself or herself, the important issue when working with a coach is to ensure you can work well together and develop an open, trusting and mutually respectful relationship. In many instances, bosses provide coaching support, and this can often be successful; however, you must be aware of the implications of having the boss as a coach: for instance, impact on promotion, performance review discussions, and so on.

The role of a coach is not to tell you what to do but, rather, to support and challenge you. In order to get the best out of any coaching relationship, you must have a purpose and objectives to work with. It really is no good simply getting a coach to help you without a purpose or objectives. A good coach will always want to know what your goals and objectives are for the relationship before agreeing to work with you. Some people find it useful to work with the same coach over many years, calling on him or her as and when necessary, while others have many different coaching relationships, often depending on the particular need at the time. In fact, we learnt that many of the women we interviewed for our previous book had had a variety of coaching relationships over the years.

Many of you told us that working with a coach has been one of the most rewarding and helpful experiences you have had in building and developing your career success.

'I have had several coaching sessions and seen huge improvement, I have worked on myself, my style and the style of my team.'

Using an external professional coach can, of course, be expensive, and therefore not available to all of you. But, this should not stop you. It can be just as beneficial to engage in a co-coaching relationship with a trusted colleague who also feels that coaching would be beneficial. If this is something that interests you, it is important to set ground rules and processes for working together, such as:

- Timing of meetings – regularity and duration
- Agree a set time and date for your next meeting every time you meet. Do not let this simply drift.
- Processes to be adopted:
  - Agree goal for session.
  - Use questioning, testing understanding, summarizing and clarification.
  - Share appropriate experiences.
  - Beware of offering advice – coaching is not about advising; it's about working together to work things through.
  - Above all, commit to complete confidentiality.

This sort of co-coaching experience is often offered during workshops and development programmes, where as part of the process the organizers set you up in coaching pairs to work together on an issue. Following the same rules and processes for real-life day-to-day coaching at work can be just as beneficial.

If this is an area that interests you, then you may like to read *The Leader's Guide to Coaching and Mentoring* by Mike Brent and Fiona Elsa Dent, which includes many tips for developing good-quality coaching and mentoring relationships.

- **A mentor** – a mentor relationship differs from a coaching relationship in that a mentor tends to be someone who is more experienced than you and who is willing to work with you to share his or her experience and knowledge and offer support and guidance. A good mentor will have many of the same skills as a coach – listening, questioning, empathizing, supporting, challenging – but will differ in that a mentor will probably focus more on job role and career development issues, rather than the broader range of development issues that you may work on with a coach.

You may also find that a mentor will offer guidance and advice, and for many people the relationship endures over many years.

US politician John Crosby summarized the relationship well in the following quote: 'Mentoring is a brain to pick, an ear to listen and a push in the right direction.'

It is also worth noting that a mentor need not be from within the organization (though for many of you he or she will probably be someone more senior than you in your organization); some people find that they identify suitable people within external environments – professional bodies, external networks, family and friends, to name a few. Don't be afraid to ask – a lot of people do.

We believe that the most successful, open and trusting mentoring relationships develop when the mentee has instigated the connection and when the relationship is not part of your direct line hierarchy. As women told us,

> 'I'm learning more now with a strong mentor whom I respect than at any point in the last 15 years'

> 'Mentoring and guidance from a senior manager with influence has helped'

'My key mentor is still influential in my life and we are good friends. She helped me a great deal and sponsored me to attend the Harvard Programme'

- **Role model** – when the women we surveyed and interviewed talked about role models, they tended to talk about those women in their organization who had reached more senior positions and who possessed the characteristics, attributes and organizational level that they themselves aspired to. Many also talked about there not being enough of them. And those who were in this position admitted that they simply could not provide support for everyone.

  'Hardly any women role models in my field or not enough around at the top to look up to.'

  'There are not enough of us (women) in top senior management and board level positions to act as role models for others'

  An additional perspective on role models that seems to be emerging is that, increasingly, role models are not simply people you can look up to and aspire to be like but, rather, people who can encourage and inspire and who can empathize with your situation: often someone who has experienced similar challenges and issues to those you are facing. Many women mention family members as being important role models, mainly as people who have supported, encouraged and inspired them. So, give it a bit of thought: who are your role models? And, remember, they are not simply famous women or those who have already made it! (Though, of course, they may be among your role models.)

  It is also worth mentioning that if you reach the dizzy heights of success, please remember to be a role model for other women. It seems from our research that there are still 'queen bees' who forget to do this.

- **Sponsor** – by a sponsor, what we mean is a person or various people who are in a position to endorse you, your capabilities and your potential to others; someone who recognizes your talents, ambitions and abilities and is willing to talk about this with relevant others as a way of helping you to build your reputation and credibility.

  So, for instance, it might be someone who is in a good position to have more knowledge than you about career or development opportunities.

Often, their role is to sow seeds for you with other key stakeholders. This could be by mentioning something you may have achieved that gives you the experience to take on a role that will be more stretching, or to put you in line for a promotion that you may not have been aware of yourself. Sometimes, you may find that this person is also your mentor or a manager whom you have worked for at some point.

'I have been lucky to have mentors, sponsors and amazing bosses who are still part of my active network now.'

Reflection. You may find it useful to reflect back over your career so far and try to identify any individuals who have sponsored you in the past. And, who might be doing it now? It is also worth noting that in this area, you must never solely rely on a sponsor to get noticed or promoted. Many people have found this out the hard way when the sponsor falls out of favour or leaves the organization, and suddenly they are afloat without a life support – the result can be derailment!

So, if you don't have a coach, mentor or sponsor in your working life at the moment, find one!

- **Learning support groups** – sometimes called action learning groups – are small groups of like-minded people who meet together on a regular basis. In our experience, this type of learning support process is much underused in business. Learning support groups are set up during development programmes but tend to fizzle out once people are back into the hurly-burly of day-to-day work and life. This is a great pity, as these sorts of groups can be incredibly beneficial for support and development. They also help provide you with a wider network of contacts than only working with individuals in your immediate workplace.

A typical learning support group will comprise a group of peers who have committed to working together, usually to explore issues that are affecting them here and now, but in reality the agenda and purpose can be whatever the group wish them to be. A typical process runs as follows:

- At the beginning, the group agree a process to work to – frequency of meetings, venue, process to operate, involving a facilitator or not.

- Focus on one group member at a time (you usually need at least thirty minutes per member), who shares with the group the issue they wish to explore and then describes it in some detail.
- The role of the others in the group is to ask questions to help the speaker reach a deeper and more rounded understanding of the issue to enable them to work through options, make decisions and plan for action.
- Group members should avoid giving advice, passing judgment or relating the speaker's situation to their own as it is important to remain focused on the speaker's situation while it is their turn.
- At the end of each person's turn, you should encourage them to summarize what they have learnt and what they plan to do.
- It may also be useful to spend time at the beginning of each meeting reviewing what people have achieved since you last met. There is little point in simply creating a therapeutic talking shop where people just share their issues – the real benefit is in what they do about them and the learning that can be gleaned from this.

The above is simply a suggestion about process; the best groups develop their own process to suit their members and their personalities and needs. One of the women we interviewed talked about a group she had set up in her organization.

'I set up a work based challenge and support female network – a small group of women who meet regularly to talk about work and the challenges and opportunities we face. This is a self motivated group who challenge and support one another.'

- **Other networks** – there are many other networks out there that can provide support, challenge and information to assist you in many different ways. For instance:

  - Groups attached to professional bodies. These can be useful in many ways. These often include specialist groups, for instance, 'Women in the Media', 'Women in Technology', 'City Women Network' and, of course, the '30% Club'. These and many other groups are worth investigating.
  - Local networks often associated with local trade groups or Chambers of Commerce.

- Groups set up on the internet with the intention of making contact with like-minded others and sharing information. For instance, there are many interest groups available on LinkedIn.

As far as sources of help are concerned, it is important that you find support mechanisms and people that work for you. For instance, some women like working with a coach but dislike the bigger networking events involved in professional groups, while others feel the opposite way. It really does not matter; the issue here is that you don't need to do it alone. There are always support possibilities; you just have to seek them out.

There are lots of other ways to get ideas, help and advice from others. Books are a great source of ideas. For instance:

- In her book *Thrive: The Third Metric to Redefining Success and Creating a Life of Well-Being, Wisdom and Wonder*, Adriana Huffington has written a deeply personal book about the challenges and demands of a successful career for a working mother.
- Duncan Bannatyne has written an excellent book, *Wake Up and Change Your Life*, about setting up your own business – and as he explains, he moved from having nothing at the age of thirty to being a millionaire at the age of thirty-seven.
- Reid Hoffman (co-founder of LinkedIn) and Ben Casnocha have written an interesting book about how to apply the principles of successful entrepreneurship to your career, *The Start-Up of You*.

It is also worth reading not only books by famous people about their journey but also books about issues that seem to affect women's careers. For instance:

- *Nice Girls Still Don't Get the Corner Office: Unconscious Mistakes Women Make That Sabotage Their Careers* by Lois P. Frankel – a practical book full of ideas on how you can succeed.
- *Mrs Moneypenny's Careers Advice for Ambitious Women* by Heather McGregor – loads of advice, tips and ideas for career success.

Like everything else we suggest, books are a very personal area, so why not search the internet or pop into a bookshop and find those that work for you?

Making it happen

Most of the women we interviewed and many of the survey comments indicated that waiting to be noticed and for things to happen simply doesn't work. Proactivity and positive action seem to be the secret. When we asked women for the advice they would give their younger self, the advice wasn't particularly age specific: Gen Y, Gen X and baby boomers all had many similar views. Taking more risks, following your dreams, being more structured, taking responsibility earlier, going for it, being bold, following your instincts, taking a chance, doing something you enjoy, and most often having more confidence and self-belief to go for what you want were common themes.

Typical comments include:

'Manage your destiny in a more structured way'

'Follow the dream, go for the career you really want'

'Self belief, be less emotional, have vision of where you want to end up and stay true to that vision'

'Stop making excuses about lack of ability and try it.'

'Take a risk. Don't worry about having a planned out life and doing things in the "right" order.'

'Three simple rules in life, 1. If you do not go after what you want you will never have it. 2. If you do not ask the answer will always be NO. 3. If you do not step forward you will always be in the same place.'

'Fear of the unknown and fear of failing will only hinder you! Try to learn as much as possible from experienced peers and supervisors without losing touch with your own skill set and true self. Stay calm in the boat when it is rocking ...'

'Be tenacious. Manage your work/home balance. Make sure you enjoy what you're doing – if it's not interesting and engaging, it's time to change'

'Don't take it personally when somebody attacks you and learn to be an assertive communicator without coming across as aggressive. And, sometimes, you just will not win, so cut your losses and use your energy to seek out something better.'

'Given the circumstance – culture, country, business, I could not have done much better. With my current experience I would perhaps move a bit faster and be less hesitant and less perfect, but all in all, the life I have now is absolutely brilliant.'

'Don't get a cat or a boyfriend – emotional ties hold you back. Stay single and go to university. Also I would say "dress for the job you want, not the job you have".'

'Be self-motivated and take opportunities. Consider your options carefully. Also one piece of advice that was given to me in my 20s which I would now like to pass onto other younger women, and originated from the female Chief Executive of the London Borough I worked in during the 1980s. She said – "When applying for a job, look at the job description (JD) as a man would. A man tends to look at a JD and says I can do that, I can do that etc., a woman often looks at a JD and high-lights the areas she can't do." So the advice from that is think positive and focus on your strengths, no one is perfect and we all need to learn skills as we progress in our careers.'

'I would advise my younger self to believe in myself more and open my mind to the art of the possible. I would try and ensure that I got access to inspirational leaders who could guide and help me earlier in my career. I would share the knowledge that it is better to try and fail than never to try at all. I would also say to be true to yourself and it is all right to walk away from something or someone if it is not making you feel good about yourself. Finally, I would say that if you can put yourself into the shoes of others and understand what it is like to be there, you have more chance to build great relationships that will be mutually rewarding. Intellect is one thing, but emotional intelligence and intuition can take someone a long way and people remember if you take time to help them on your journey. It is also personally satisfying when you can make that difference.'

Reflection. It seems to us that the first challenge is knowing what you want from your work. Here are some practical ideas for strategizing and coaching yourself for your career future. Do a quick review of your level of satisfaction with where you are now by completing the following:

20 Questions about your career			
	Audit question	**Yes/No/ Not sure**	**Notes**
1	Are you happy with your job, role, career at the moment?		
2	Do you enjoy your job?		
3	Is your job intellectually satisfying?		
4	Does your work make you feel anxious or depressed?		
5	Do you feel there is room to grow and develop in your current job?		
6	Are you working too many hours each week?		
7	Do you feel you are suffering from work overload?		
8	Do you have someone to help deal with work pressures?		
9	Do you feel that you are in control of your career?		
10	Do you feel that you have purpose in your career?		
11	Are you confident in your abilities at work?		
12	Do you have skills and capabilities that you are not currently using?		
13	Do you know what your next career move is likely to be? In two years, five years, etc....		
14	Do you feel recognized for your work?		

15	Is your pay and reward package fair and equitable (in relation to male colleagues)?		
16	Are you happy in your working environment?		
17	Do you work for a supportive boss?		
18	Do you have supportive colleagues?		
19	Do your family and friends support you?		
20	Are you happy overall?		
Summary Notes, Insights, Ideas			

Summary

Our view is that you should regularly review your career, and it's often surprising how long people will wait before making time to do this. Much of the career advice and ways of coaching yourself will also apply to men – lots of topics are gender neutral. But women's careers also differ in some respects. An obvious one that we hear often is that women think far more about the reasons why they **should not** take an opportunity rather than thinking about **why they should**. If you take nothing else from this book, then please remember 'Five Good Reasons Why' and apply it to the rest of your career. It will make a difference!

You should also be aware that some women sabotage their own careers. An example that's been recently featured in the press is about the pay differential – this often starts in the first job and continues through each level, with a large gap at the most senior levels. Men are perhaps better at negotiating and 'asking' and women are more accepting. For instance, as Sheryl Sandberg told us in her book *Lean In*, she accepted the first offer that Mark Zuckerberg made when joining Facebook. When she told the good news to her family, her male relatives suggested that she might get a better deal if she did what many men would do – negotiate! And she did.

Another good example of this is hesitancy. Whether this is part of social conditioning or more about our personality, cultural and family preferences is not important here. What is crucial is that individual women are aware of it and recognize when they behave in this way. It may seem simply polite to say 'I'd just like to ask ...' or 'this may be a silly question but can I point out that ...', but the way we use language means that others around us will make assumptions. Instead, use clearer, more direct phrases such as 'Let me ask ...' or 'Let me point out that ...'

Finally, Americans sometimes use the term 'savvy' about someone who is smart and clever about getting what they want. We hope you will be career savvy and remember that although luck does often play a part in success, strategizing and taking responsibility for yourself is much more important.

'Have a plan – for this year, for the next 18 months, for the next 3 years. Be conscious about the steps you make to ensure you remain marketable and up to date'

'Don't be scared to leave a company to progress and follow your dreams – take your career management into your own hands and a level of uncertainty is OK.'

Chapter 10

The current landscape for working women

Previous chapters in this book are about **YOU** and your career, but this chapter sets out to outline the bigger picture. What exactly is happening for working women at the moment, and what was the journey for women in earlier generations? So, we shall start off with what's happening here and now.

In some respects, the situation for working women has never been better. You can decide to start your own company, go into politics, business, law, academic life, accountancy, medicine, marketing, or pretty much any area. The horizon for many women today is far brighter than it was for earlier generations of women, but yet ... let's begin with a couple of stories.

> One woman is a senior manager with a large hi-tech company that she joined from university. She has gradually moved up over the years in terms of responsibility and budgets that she looks after. Yet, when she compares her own career with those of male colleagues, she notices a clear disconnect – they have received greater awards and a few more promotions (not to mention bonuses). It's hard to pin down the reasons why this has happened – it's certainly not down to different levels of drive and ambition. And, a few years ago, when she went on maternity leave, her start-up project was taken over by an assistant she had recruited. When she returned a few months later, she found that she was expected to report to him!
> **Senior manager, tech industry, who is in her 30s.**

> 'I count myself fortunate as I've recently graduated and landed a great job in a really exciting industry. It couldn't be better but I notice that while there are women here among my colleagues when I look above my level I see few women. Hardly any are part of the different senior management teams.'
> **Project leader, pharma, who is in her 20s.**

Both these situations are real and illustrate the sort of experiences we regularly heard about from working women. Sometimes women are judged differently from men; something that can happen in small-, medium- and large-sized firms. We meet hundreds of working women each year in the course of our teaching, consultancy, coaching and research work. Some are working in the public sector, while others are based in large private-sector firms, and across many different industry sectors and continents we hear about similar situations. There are, no doubt, some outstandingly good employers working hard to create great workplaces for women, but this is not yet true in the majority of businesses.

Sometimes, it is the working environment that is not 'women-friendly'. A professional firm recently investigated the reasons why women did not progress to partner level. One of the issues identified was the lack of career choices; many women felt that it counted against them, for promotion and advancement, if they did not want to work the excessively long hours that were the 'norm' across all areas of the business.

Another large employer in the finance sector was recently shocked to find that a number of women in their 30s who were leaving were not stopping work to be full-time mothers. This is what the company had assumed. Instead, these women were voting with their feet against the tough macho culture in the business and were moving to other, more family-friendly and women-friendly employers where they could find more support and encouragement for their careers.

Some of the most likely career issues that are mentioned when coaching women are:

- Dealing with a macho culture with a tough (sometimes bullying) management style. Often, the focus is on 'task' and can exclude or ignore the 'people' issues.
- No role models: a number of industries have few women at middle or senior management levels. In some disciplines – such as microelectronics – there are few women to be found at any level. In a large-scale survey conducted by 'Opportunity Now', a group of women aged from 28 to 40 were asked about role models. Over half of respondents said that there were few role models at their workplace.
- Lack of confidence.
- Work–life balance: juggling the job with family or personal issues.

- No immediate opportunities for promotion.
- A patronizing attitude from older, more senior male managers.
- Dual-career issues – moving geographical area or the problems of combining family responsibilities with two careers.

Reflection. You might like to consider at this point what your response would be to a couple of typical coaching questions:

> What's it like being a woman in your company/your profession?
> And, do you feel that you face particular barriers because you are a woman?

We'll return to this current landscape shortly, but first, we'd like to tell you a little bit about how things have changed for different generations of working women. We apologize to any of our readers who may already know this or to those of you who usually find history rather boring. However, it's a story that's far from boring, and we'd like to tell you about the extraordinary journey that working women have made. Some of the first women to study at Cambridge University would pretend to go into a cake shop to buy cakes – just in case people would notice that they were attending classes. In fact, there were even public demonstrations against admitting women as university graduates, and some of the male professors who tutored in those early days also had to keep a low profile.

If we go back far enough, there was a time when women from earlier generations were excluded from university or the civil service; nor could they enter any of the professions, such as law, medicine or accountancy. A decision made simply because of gender. Women could not vote and had no right to a university education; there were no women MPs, and no women held ministerial roles in the government. There were no female barristers or judges, and not a single woman was eligible to practise law until 1922, when Ivy Williams graduated. Ivy Williams also became the first woman to teach law at a UK university. And, just in case you think this is all about events back in the early twentieth century, a marriage bar existed until the 1970s in parts of the civil service. Women were expected to resign when they married.

Until the equal pay legislation in the 1970s, it was possible, and legal, for companies to pay different wages depending on gender. This usually meant that women were paid less – there may be instances where men were paid less, but neither of us knows of any examples. If you've seen the film *Made in Dagenham* (2010), it's a good example of what took place. A current ongoing case about equal pay involves a major UK supermarket. But let's stick with the 1970s for a while.

From the 1970s to the twenty-first century

Eleanor Macdonald is not a very well-known name these days, but she really does deserve greater fame. She died at the age of ninety-three in 2004 and was a determined, opinionated and delightful person who loved a challenge: qualities that were very useful for her campaign in founding a group called 'Women in Management' back in 1969. She felt that women did not get a fair deal, and, together with a number of other pioneering women, set up a network to help address this problem. They needed more support, more encouragement, and most of all, more tools and techniques to help them build their career. Most women working in those days were likely to be secretaries, nurses or shop assistants, and very few set their sights on becoming managers. Being a manager was definitely seen by most as being a man's job rather than 'women's work'. A woman manager was a novel idea, and people (men and women alike) might say they did not want to work for a woman manager. So, perhaps you can appreciate how much has changed since then?

A European network with similar aspirations was founded in 1984: 'the European Women's Management Development Network'. Conferences were hosted in different countries each year, and Hamburg, Stockholm, Barcelona, Zurich, Amsterdam, Brighton and Milan were among the cities hosting these early events. The publicity, and women's need for such support, often meant that local membership would explode after such a national meeting. This was especially true in Germany, where within a short space of time, a variety of regional networks were launched. What was interesting was how much similarity there was between the issues for women in the different countries. Things had changed since 1969, and there were more women managers, but still in the late 1980s (and also through the 1990s) it was possible to attend business meetings where there might be only a few women, a token woman or often no women at all. The same was true in government and diplomatic life, where women were similarly scarce.

It was not until Veronica Sutherland became ambassador to the Ivory Coast in 1987 that a married woman was appointed; every previous British female ambassador had been unmarried and childless. We talk quite often these days about whether women can 'have it all' and be career women as well as mothers: countless women in the 1970s and 1980s deliberately selected their career instead of marriage and family, and some still do!

But, slowly, change did happen. Two amazing changes occurred in very different spheres – politics and space. The political seismic shift happened when a woman was appointed as leader of a major party and then, from 1979 for just over a decade until 1990, as prime minister. Her name, of course, was Margaret Thatcher.

The space breakthrough has been rather forgotten in comparison. In 1991, the first British astronaut in space was a woman! Helen Sharman, who had been a chemist for the Mars chocolate company, was selected from a field of nearly 13,000 applicants, and all the newspapers reported her achievements in great detail. She spent a year preparing for her trip into space, and her space suit had to be made for her – she recently commented that it's still the only suit that has ever been tailor-made for her!

So, there is no doubt that the situation for working women was changing, and this has continued. There are now more women in science and many more graduates. A greater number of women hold junior and middle management appointments, but women are still too infrequently found at senior levels or as directors in the boardroom. The same is true in other areas. While, for example, there may be more women politicians at local and national levels, few of the most senior roles are held by women. We may have had one woman prime minister, but there has not yet been another, and there is still not equality at every level. This means that across the working world, there are too few role models for younger women to encourage and inspire them. And, an important point for younger women is that there are too few role models of working mothers.

A large number of those who responded to our survey commented on how challenging it is to combine family and career, and many of them 'opt out' by not returning after their first maternity break or when a second baby arrives. Carolyn McCall, chief executive of EasyJet, acknowledges the problems, and has set in place initiatives within EasyJet to create a more female-friendly environment, including mentoring for younger women who are setting out on their career and looking at ways to increase (and maintain) the number of female pilots.

Female firsts and milestones

There also are still plenty of 'firsts' in which a woman is holding a post for the first time, as shown in the recent examples below. The final example, at Oxford University, is definitely a historic event, breaking the traditions of nearly 800 years.

- **2009: Anne Pringle** was the first female British ambassador to Moscow since diplomatic links were first established 450 years ago.
- **2010: Professor Dame Sally Davies** was appointed as the chief medical officer for England, the first woman to fill this post.
  (We interviewed Dame Sally Davies for our earlier book *Women in Business: Navigating Career Success*.)
- **2013:** Forty years after the first woman entered the Lloyd's of London dealing floor as a broker, the 325-year-old insurance market named its first female chief executive, **Inga Beale**.
  Marjorie Scardino, previously CEO of media firm Pearson, was appointed to the board of Twitter following criticism of an all-male

board. (Marjorie Scardino was the first female CEO of a FTSE 100 firm in 1997.) **Sharon White** became the first woman appointed as a permanent secretary at the Treasury.

- **2014: Laura Wade-Gery** was promoted to lead Marks & Spencer's 800 UK stores as part of a revamp of the board. She is the first woman to lead the M&S retail business, and joined the board in 2011.
- **2015:** Deloitte named veteran **Cathy Engelbert** as chief executive officer, making her the first woman to become CEO of a major US accounting and consulting firm. She joined the company in 1986. **Louise Richardson**, appointed as vice chancellor at Oxford University, is the first woman to hold this position in nearly 800 years! It's also interesting to note that when Professor Richardson joined the University of St Andrews in 2009, she was the only woman in the senior team.

You may also be interested to learn some other milestones for working women. We've divided these up into time capsules to highlight the different decades.

Fifty years of milestones for working women

In the 1960s

1964   Mary Kendrick is the first woman to receive the Institution of Civil Engineer's Thomas Telford gold medal for her work – and led the early fieldwork into the Thames Barrier.

1969   'Women in Management' is founded.

In the 1970s

1970   Equal pay legislation in the UK. **Barbara Castle**, the MP who was responsible for bringing in this Act, was a keen supporter of women's rights.

1976   Anne Warburton is the first female British ambassador. She served as British ambassador to Denmark from 1976 to 1983.
Divina Galica is the first woman to compete in Formula 1 racing. There have only been five female drivers in Formula 1 – including, more recently, **Susie Wolff** who joined the Williams team in 2014.

1979   Margaret Thatcher is the first (and still the only) woman prime minister in the UK.

In the 1980s

1982   Harriet Harman is elected as one of only ten female Labour MPs in parliament.

1983   Janet Thomson, a scientist, is finally allowed on a research ship for Antarctica, becoming the first woman to work inside the Antarctic Circle. She had argued her case for eighteen years before finally winning the argument that women could work on the research stations.

Mary Donaldson is the first woman elected as Lord Mayor of the City of London.

1984   The 'European Women's Management Development Network' is launched. Based in Brussels, the country networks quickly develop to include the UK, France, Germany, Belgium, Holland, Spain, Switzerland and Italy.

Beverly Lynn Burns is the first woman captain of a Boeing 747 jumbo jet (on 18 July, to be precise, on a flight from Newark to Los Angeles). She was a role model for many young American women. **Brenda Dean** is the first woman elected to head a major trade union in the UK.

1985   Sian Griffiths becomes one of Britain's first female firefighters.

1987   Thousands are inspired by **Diane Abbott** when she became the first black female MP in 1987.

In the 1990s

1991   The RAF's first female pilot is **Julie Ann Gibson**. Women did fly planes in the Second World War, and they could serve in the Women's Auxiliary Air Force (WAAF). (To read more about those earlier times, see *Spitfire Women of World War II*, written in 2008 by Giles Whittell.)

1992   (to 2000) Betty Boothroyd is the first, and so far the only, woman elected as speaker in the House of Commons.

Stella Rimington is the first woman director general of MI5 (until 1996), and also the first director general whose name was published when she was appointed.

1993   Karren Brady appointed managing director of Birmingham City Football Club.

1994   Jo Salter is the first female operational fast jet pilot – flying Tornados with 617 Squadron.

1995   Pauline Clare in Lancashire is appointed chief constable and is the first woman to hold this job.

Alison Hargreaves is the first woman to climb Mount Everest alone and without oxygen. She died later that year attempting to climb K2, one of the world's most difficult mountains.

1997   Marjorie Scardino at Pearson is the first female CEO in a leading UK firm (in the FTSE 100).

1998   Heather Hallett is the first woman to chair the Bar Council, which represents barristers in England and Wales.

1999   Clara Freeman is the first woman appointed to the board at Marks & Spencer.

In the 2000s and after

2000   *Management Today* magazine launches the thirty-five Women Under thirty-five awards. Still going strong, the awards reached their fifteenth anniversary in 2015.

2001   **Clara Furse** is the first woman chief executive at the London Stock Exchange (until 2009).

2005   Athena SWAN Charter was launched to encourage the careers of women in (STEMM) areas – science, technology, engineering, maths and medicine.

2009   **Kirsty Moore** is the first female pilot in the Red Arrows team (2009–2012).

2010   The '30% Club' is launched – aiming to persuade leading UK firms (FTSE 100) to appoint more women to board level, moving towards a 30 per cent goal. **Nancy Rothwell** is the first woman vice chancellor at the University of Manchester – the UK's biggest university.
Kathryn Bigelow is the first woman to win the 'best director' award at the Oscars. This was for her low-budget war film about Iraq, *The Hurt Locker*.

2012   **Debbie Jevans** is appointed director of sport for the Olympic Games 2012. She was formerly a professional tennis player and is now chief executive officer England Rugby (2015). **Adeline Ginn** founded 'Women in Rail' to provide support and networking opportunities, as well as promoting the industry as an attractive career choice for other women: see 'Being a woman isn't a barrier to working in the rail industry' at http://www.theguardian.com/women-in-leadership/2015/may/15/being-a-woman-isnt-a-barrier-to-working-in-the-rail-industry.

2014   **Princess Anne** is the first woman invited to join the Royal and Ancient Golf Club of St Andrews. In **2015**, golfers **Laura Davies, Renée Powell, Belle Robertson, Louise Suggs, Lally Segard and Annika Sorenstam** also accepted invitations to become honorary members. The club's 2,400 members voted by 85 per cent to admit women for the first time in its 260-year history.
Susie Wolff (mentioned earlier) is the first woman to take part in a Formula 1 race in twenty-two years at Silverstone at the British Grand Prix.

2015   Following the 2015 UK general election, the number of women in parliament has risen by a third. It is the biggest increase since 1997. Of the 650 seats, approximately 29 per cent of MPs, and nearly half of all Labour MPs, are women. Previously, women held 23 per cent of all the seats. However, not everything is good – the UK Independence Party (UKIP), the Liberal Democrats and the Democratic Unionist Party (DUP) have no female MPs, and some parties had no female candidates. **Mhairi Black** was elected MP for Paisley and Renfrewshire South in 2015 at age twenty, which makes her the youngest MP elected to the House of Commons since at least the Reform Act of 1832. Both major political parties in Scotland are now led by women – **Nicola Sturgeon** leads the Scottish Nationalist Party and **Kezia Dugdale** leads the Scottish Labour Party. **Dame Zaha Mohammad Hadid DBE**, an Iraqi-British architect who designed, among other things, the Sheikh Zayed Bridge in Abu Dhabi and the Riverside Museum in Glasgow and has won the contract to build the stadium for the 2020 Tokyo Olympics, is the first woman to win the Royal Institute of British Architects gold medal.

Women in chief executive officer roles

It is also true that, while there are now more female chief executives, there are not very many, nor are many to be found at board level, despite a vigorous debate and campaign in the UK to increase female board appointments. In fact, there is another key date – in 2010 – when Helena Morrissey decided to launch the 30 per cent Club. In much the same spirit as Eleanor Macdonald, the 30 per cent Club is action oriented and aims to inspire senior executives, chief executives and chairmen in the corporate world to seek out more of those talented women who could, and should, be in the boardroom. The goal of the 30 per cent Club is for women to hold 30 per cent of board-level appointments in leading FTSE 100 companies, and a variety of events and support mechanisms are available to help with this, including mentoring.

With regard to female chief executives, it is probably worthwhile saying pre-cisely what we mean when we say that there are 'not very many'. As at March 2015, twenty-three of the Fortune 500 companies in the United States had a female chief executive. In the UK's leading companies – those in the FTSE 250 – there were only sixteen female chief executives. Right at the top of the tree, among FTSE 100 leading companies listed on the UK stock exchange as at May 2015, the number is six! There could have been one more if Marjorie Scardino, at Pearson, had remained in post for another year. Back in 1997, she was the first woman to head up a FTSE 100 company and built an impressive business at Pearson, tripling the profits. Not only does the company now own most of Penguin Random publishing and a half stake in the *Economist* magazine, but it has grown to be one of the largest educa-tion publishing and testing businesses worldwide. More recently, in 2013, Marjorie Scardino was the first woman appointed to the board of Twitter – the company had been widely criticized for having an all-male board.

It's also worth looking at the senior levels of certain professions. In law, for example, there are twenty-one women who are High Court judges (among 108), seven women who sit in the Court of Appeal (among 38), and one woman, Baroness Hale, in the Supreme Court (among 12).

Another indicator of the scarcity of women in business came in early 2015 when the *Financial Times* newspaper published a list of fifty leading busi-ness pioneers. The list featured those who have set trends, started com-panies and sometimes earned significant sums of money along the way. Readers might have expected to find a considerable number of women included on this list, and you might like to speculate at this point what would be a reasonable number to find: would ten be too low? Would twenty be more likely, or perhaps even more?

In fact, there are only six women on the list – all of whom are working in fashion and beauty. This seems a tiny number, and reveals the fact that there are still too few women both in the corporate world and as entrepreneurs who are running their own companies.

International comparisons

You may be wondering how the UK is doing compared with other countries. The evidence suggests that while our record is reasonable, we are certainly not leaders. The UK is at its highest position since 2000 on the 2013 index 'Women in Work' compiled by consultants Price Waterhouse Coopers (PwC). The UK ranks fourteenth out of twenty-seven developed economies – it was eighteenth in the previous survey a year earlier.

Women in work index – UK, US and Hungary rise. Australia, Portugal, Poland and Ireland fall

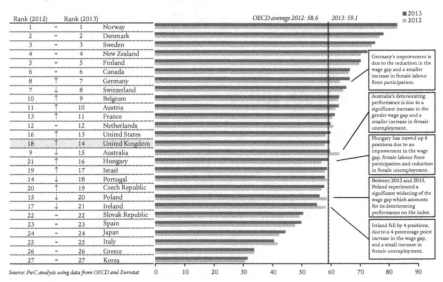

www.pwc.co.uk/the-economy/publications/women-in-work-index.jhtml
Published with permission from PwC.

Internationally, there is more interest these days, with more comparative data available about working women. In fact, many organizations worldwide publish their own reviews. This is very good news compared with, say, ten years ago, when there was far less interest in such topics. A number of recent studies illustrate some key issues and echo many similar findings to those we mentioned in our earlier book, as briefly outlined below. We also surveyed women for this book – and are grateful to the organizations, individuals and networks who helped us circulate the survey.

Back in the 1990s, the European Union held a number of workshops to review the situation for women in media, radio and broadcasting, and looked at various ways to encourage women to see this as a career option. However, it's important to look at both sides. It is not only about who is reporting and writing about our society, but also about who is on the other side – presenting programmes, 'on camera' and being interviewed. You might like to think about a report by the Fawcett Society published in 2013. This research found that in a typical month, about 72 per cent of the BBC *Question Time* programme contributors, and 84 per cent of reporters and guests on the BBC Radio 4 *Today* programme, were men. If this happened occasionally – say for one month of the year – and for the rest of the time gender was more balanced, that would be an interesting fact. However, if it is a continuing trend, then clearly it is wrong, as it does not reflect the number of talented women who could be included.

Women at work today

This has been a quick and very brief tour of some of the issues, and some of the changes for working women. To summarize, there are some positive encouraging changes, but women still receive lower pay and far fewer of the top jobs. There is also the issue of sexism. For more on this, read Laura Bates' website and weekly blog 'Everyday Sexism'. She also writes a weekly blog for the *Guardian* newspaper (www.theguardian.com; also see the website at http://everydaysexism.com).

The good news is that these days, women are increasingly holding leadership roles, such as Christine Lagarde at the International Monetary Fund. This is evident not only in business circles but in a variety of key industries, such as fashion and other areas. Anna Wintour, for example, has edited the *American Vogue* magazine for over twenty years, and is highly influential in the fashion world. She is also artistic director at Condé Nast, the publishers of *Vogue*. In politics, Nicola Sturgeon was elected leader of the Scottish Nationalist Party. But there remains some far less positive news, such as the low numbers of women at senior executive and board level, and the continuing pay gap – this exists in every country, including the United States, and is wider at more senior levels.

Additionally, women these days are now able to work at the Antarctic British research stations. Until twenty years ago, women were banned, but today, on average, a third of those working at Rothera – the largest station – will be women. Marine biologist Mairi Fenton recalls what happened for her parents (back in the 1970s). Her father, a biologist, joined the station, but her mother, a scientist, could not because of the 'no women' rule.

On a less positive note, women are still more likely to work in business support functions such as PR, HR and marketing. Although these jobs can be a stepping stone to senior and CEO roles, they are far less likely to be in comparison with finance, international and operational appointments.

Stereotypes about women continue. A recent online kerfuffle was about whether women are too emotional to be involved in science! A particularly important issue is about leadership styles and stereotypes – for example, a more people-focused approach by a woman may be seen as soft and fluffy, but if a man uses this style, it might well be labelled as an inclusive and coaching style. Likewise, a strong leadership style might be good for a man but seen as aggressive in a woman. These are often unconscious stereotypes that we may hold and rarely discuss with others.

Both in the media and in our own research, it appears that for working mothers, there is still a reluctance by employers to enable part-time working in senior roles. Part-time is regarded as something more relevant for more junior roles. There are also mistaken stereotypes, such as that a working mother will not want a career, and these unspoken assumptions can be toxic in terms of succession planning discussions and talent management processes in larger companies. The media's influence is particularly interesting with regard to the stereotypes about mothers. The 2015 winner of the Veuve Clicquot 'businesswoman of the year' award,

Katherine Garrett-Cox, chief executive of Alliance Trust, was described in one newspaper article as 'a mother of 4 children'. As someone quickly pointed out, men are rarely described as 'a father of 4'.

There are many, many areas in which women undoubtedly have made progress – the House of Commons and the political arena, for example. But there remain many other places where progress is exceedingly slow. You may like to scan some recent headlines from newspaper and journal articles, which highlight both the positive and negative, as these demonstrate the issues that still occur for women.

Spotlight: Women and women's issues in the media

'The Truth about Queen Bee Bosses' – *Times*, 9 June 2015

'Number of Women Working in Digital Industries Decrease' – *HR Review* 10 June 2015 (UK Commission for Employment & Skills)

'One in Five Believe Women Can't Reach Senior Management' – *HR Magazine*, 7 August 2015

'Females Not Hopeful for Career Progression in Financial Sector' – *HR Review* 10 June 2015 (A report by PwC. PriceWaterhouseCoopers)

'Male Lawyers Receive Bonuses 66% Higher than Females' – *HR Review*, 11 June 2015

'Women Still Face a Glass Ceiling' – *Guardian*, 21 February 2011

'Entrenched Macho Work Cultures Deter Talented Female Applicants, Finds Survey' – *People Management*, 26 May 2015

'What's Holding Women Back?' – *Economist*, 23 January 2015

'London: Sexism and the City' – *Financial Times*, 16 January 2015

'Where Did All the Women Go?' – *Grocer*, 13 August 2007

'FTSE 100 Attracts Chief Execs from All over the World – but Women are Still a Rarity at the Top' – *Daily Telegraph*, 20 May 2015

'Female Pilots: A Slow Take-off' – *Guardian*, 13 January 2014

'Video Games on the Gender Agenda: Women in the Gaming Industry Talk about Being in a Minority and Their Optimism for More Girls Choosing It as a Career' – *Financial Times*, 5 June 2015

'Stop Blaming Women: Prescribing a 21st Century Approach to Gender Diversity' – Hay Group Report, 2013

'Male Bonuses Double Those of Women' – *BBC News*, 20 August 2015

'We Just Don't Do Schlock: Why Women are Kept from the Heights of the Movie World' – *Guardian*, 20 June 2015

'Why a Baby Can Still Ruin Your Career' – *Daily Telegraph*, 25 July 2015

'Is There Sexism in Science Labs?' *Inside Science* – BBC Radio 4, first broadcast 18 June 2015

'Where Are All the Women Creative Directors?' by Lydia Dishman, www.fastcompany.com, 26 February 2013

'A Third of Women Say Men Are Offered More Opportunities at Work' by Katie Jacobs, *HR Magazine*, 3 June 2015

'5 Myths Keeping Women out of Science Careers' by Yvonne Baker, *Guardian*, 5 March 2015

'Parenthood and Academia: An Impossible Balance?' *Times Higher Education*, 4 September 2014

'Britain Failing to Build Bridges with Women' by Edward Curwen, *Times*, 22 June 2015

'Man City Rules: Only 1 in 10 Fund Managers Is a Woman' by Ali Hussain, *Sunday Times*, 19 July 2015

'Why British Women Need a Diplomatic Coup' by Sue Cameron, *Daily Telegraph*, 9 August 2014

'Half of Employees Say Employers Discriminate against Working Mothers', *HR Today Online*, 8 September 2015

'Pay Rise for Nearly Third of Female Workers', *Guardian*, 3 September 2015 (This refers to how the rise in the living wage will benefit women most! They make the point that women tend to be clustered in low-paid jobs.)

'Taylor Swift Can Teach British Women a Lesson: Unlike Their Ballsy US Counterparts, Too Many Women Here Opt Out of High-Flying Careers and Don't Become Role Models', *Times*, 24 June 2015

Reflection. Why not think about your own environment and assess your company/sector using the following statements in the quiz below? If you are freelancer, or running your own enterprise, then think back over the past few weeks and consider how the people you meet in your working life treat you. Have you experienced sexist behaviour? Is your organization female-friendly? How much support and career advice do you receive from your manager and from your HR Department? Is it easy to find out about promotion opportunities within your part of the business? Do men's and women's careers in your organization progress at the same speed?

Organization analysis: 10 key questions

Statement	True	False	Don't know
Men and women are equally likely to be promoted here			
My organization makes it easy to combine a career with family responsibilities			
Working mothers are treated equally			
Training opportunities are equally distributed by gender			
There is no pay gap here between male and female salaries (or bonus payments)			

My organization is part of the '50% Group' (A place where there is a 50:50 gender split at each level of seniority)			
There are policies here to attract women returners; for example, Deloitte has a twelve-week 'Return to Work' programme for women who previously worked for the firm			
Part-time people here have the same career opportunities as those who work full time			
There are some negative stereotypes about women managers in my organization, for example, a man is assumed to be a good manager but a woman has to prove she is good			
There are female role models in senior positions in my organization			

Your notes/observations on your replies above:

Considering these issues will also help you when you are joining a new employer. It is worth asking questions around some of these issues during the recruitment process to determine how female-friendly the organization currently is. For instance: 'What's the gender balance at senior level? And, what does the organization do to help working parents?' If you get the feeling at the recruitment stage that the environment is not female-friendly, then it may mean that life for working women will be more difficult. And some words to finish with – from Radio 4 *Today* presenter and journalist Mishal Husain:

> Women need to keep fighting. When I was in my twenties, I thought that the feminist battle had been won, but as I grow older I realise there is still work to do. Even though young women today are much more aware of their rights and more vocal about their aspirations, there is still a pay gap and still a glass ceiling.

Conclusion

The aim of this book is to demonstrate to you the value of career coaching and strategizing: to show you ways to do this, to highlight key areas that women can use to develop their own career, and to offer practical exercises, tools and techniques to help every woman thrive and survive. We hope that we have achieved this, and that this book will offer you some insights, tips and advice to help you build a better career.

All of the exercises we've used will help you focus on what's important to you and help you understand yourself better. This knowledge can be helpful at many different career stages throughout your working life. For instance:

- when leading a team for the first time
- when returning to work following maternity leave or a longer career break
- when switching careers
- when rebooting your career!
- when applying for promotion
- when taking an international assignment

It is also true to say that corporate careers have changed in many ways over recent years, but there are still some certainties, such as:

- There will be promotions and special assignments that will add that certain something to your CV. Make sure you know what these are.
- There are too few career signposts and information to help you early on in your career. These are crucial years when if you find a great team, or a great boss, this will impact on your confidence and develop skills you didn't know you had!
- If you don't say you are ambitious, then people around you are likely to think that you are not. So, find a way of expressing this to others around you.
- Women are more likely to migrate towards certain roles – such as HR and marketing – that make it harder to have a perfect CV for a board

or CEO role. Be aware of the choices you are making. Likewise, international, finance and operational roles are often more valued. So, if you take your marketing or HR role and work internationally, this will help you tick one of the key boxes.

- It has always been beneficial to have financial and operational experience. As one of our survey respondents said, 'Get P&L experience as early as possible in your career.'

And finally, we'd like to offer you a series of top tips for success and five key factors that will help build your career.

Sixteen top tips for success

1. **Negotiate!** Whether it's about salary, promotion, workloads or work–life balance, remember the power of negotiation and do not simply accept what you are initially offered. It's also worth learning how to say 'no'.
2. Be aware of **stress, pressure and potential burnout**: there is a price to pay for working 60, 80 or even more hours each week. Learn how to be resilient.
3. Beware of **the danger of wanting to be 'perfect'**.
4. **It's never too late to change** your job, role, or sector, or to start your own business.
5. **Keep your CV up to date.** Remember, your CV can open or shut doors for you when applying for a job. You should tailor your CV for any job you apply for and ensure you use active words, such as 'achieved, negotiated, delivered, launched and won'.
6. **Have a plan for your career**, and for your life in general. It doesn't have to be adhered to rigidly, but it's a good idea to know where you want to be in two years and in five years. Set career goals and take time to understand key assignments and critical skills; think about 'how do you get ahead here?'
7. **Speak up**, contribute, step forward, volunteer: these are all key attributes you will need if you want to get noticed. Think about yourself as a brand.
8. Build your **confidence and self-esteem**.

9. **Choose your battles** wisely. Don't go into battle for every single issue in the workplace, but consider which battles are worth fighting. It's also worth pointing out that while many women say they do not like office politics – and that is understandable – you do need to be aware of them. Understand who influences whom in your company, learn about different ways to influence different people.

10. **Find supporters** to help you achieve your career – coaches, sponsors and mentors are particularly important.

11. **A good boss** who supports you (as well as challenging you) can help you develop to the next level. A bad boss will invariably hold you back, though it is possible to learn from them about what you will, and will not, do when you are the boss!

12. **Build a good team** around you. Investing in the people who work with you will pay dividends in the long run.

13. Build and develop strong and relevant relationship **networks**.

14. Earn a reputation as **someone who delivers** what they promise.

15. **Understand the principles of good coaching** – you need to set yourself challenging goals. Not impossible to reach, but challenging nevertheless.

16. **Be persistent and determined** – if you want something then don't give up at the first or the second disappointment.

Inside careers today: Five things you need to know

-   **Leave a lasting impression:** Some people will tell you that impression management is a bad thing. That may well be true if it is all about external self-promotion and 'spin' with no internal substance, but that's not what we mean. We mean 'impact'. Think about a company you deal with and who it is that has made an impression on you personally – and why. Often, they are good at what they do, but we notice that it's that extra something that makes the transaction more personal, more relevant or more efficient. This is the type of impact we mean, so think about what people would say about you. Will they single you out from your colleagues – will they ask for you to be on the project team?

- **It's all about people:** At every level in business and across our careers, it's the personal relationships that make a difference. A recent example was someone who had a call from a headhunter – was she interested in a new role with another company? No, but she did know someone who fitted their profile almost perfectly ... and they were interviewed and won the job. Would anyone recommend you?
- **Work smarter, not just harder:** You can have the best reputation in the world for being a hard worker, but you need to understand the principles of working smarter rather than just applying more hours to the job.
- **How do people get on around here?** Ask yourself and others this question, gather intelligence and knowledge – it's all about awareness.
- **Step up:** put yourself forward for new challenges, opportunities and promotions. Even if you don't get them first time, you have made the point and demonstrated your interest.

WE WISH YOU THE VERY BEST OF LUCK

Bibliography

Ahmed, A. (2015), *Worlds Apart: A Muslim Girl with the SAS*. London: Robson Press.

Angier, M. and Axelrod, B. (2014), Realizing the Power of Talented Women. *McKinsey Quarterly*, September 2014.

Bannatyne, D. (2009), *Wake Up and Change Your Life*. London: Orion.

Bingham, L. (2012), Role Models Are Essential to Help Women Reach the Top. *The Guardian*, 27 September 2012.

Brady, K. (2013), *Strong Woman, The Truth about Getting to the Top*. London: HarperCollins.

Brent, M. and Dent, F. E. (2010), *The Leader's Guide to Influence: How to Use Soft Skills to Get Hard Results*. Harlow: Pearson.

Brent, M. and Dent, F. E. (2014), *The Leader's Guide to Managing People: How to Use Soft Skills to Get Hard Results*. Harlow: Pearson.

Brent, M. and Dent, F. E. (2015), *The Leader's Guide to Coaching and Mentoring: How to Use Soft Skills to Get Hard Results*. Harlow: Pearson.

Carter, L. and Sullivan, R. L. (2013), *The Change Champion's Field Guide: Strategies and Tools for Leading Change in Your Organization*. Chichester: John Wiley and Sons.

Ceserani, J. and Hailstone, P. (2003), *The Problem Solving Pocketbook*. Alresford: Management Pocketbooks.

Chartered Management Institute (2014), *Women in Management: The Power of Role Models*. Chartered Management Institute.

Coffman, J. and Neuenfeldt, B. (2014), *Everyday Moments of Truth: Frontline Managers are Key to Women's Career Aspirations*. Bain and Company.

Dent, F. E. (2009) *Working Relationships Pocketbook*. Alresford: Management Pocketbooks.

Dent, F., Rabbetts, J. and Holton, V. (2013), *The Ashridge Management Index 2012/13*. Ashridge Business School.

Donnelly, M. (2015), The 50 Percent Club. *McKinsey Quarterly*, February 2015.

Fleming, K. (2015), *The Leader's Guide to Emotional Agility*. Harlow: Pearson.

Frankel, L. P. (2014), *Nice Girls Still Don't Get the Corner Office: Unconscious Mistakes Women Make That Sabotage Their Careers*. New York: Business Plus.

Goffman, E. (1959), *The Presentation of Self in Everyday Life*. London: Penguin.

Goleman, D. (1996), *Emotional Intelligence: Why It Can Matter More than IQ*. London: Bloomsbury.

Harvard Business Review (2015), *Women in the Workplace: A Research Roundup*. HBR.org.

Hewlett, S. A. (2007), *Off Ramps and On Ramps: Keeping Talented Women on the Road to Success*. Harvard: Harvard Business School Press.

Hoffman, R. and Casnocha, B. (2013), *The Start-Up of You: Adapt to The Future, Invest in Yourself and Transform Your Career*. New York: Random House Business.

Holton, V. and Dent, F. E. (2012), *Women in Business: Navigating Career Success*. Basingstoke: Palgrave Macmillan.

Honore, S. and Paine-Schofield, C. (2012), *Culture Shock: Generation Y and Their Managers around the World*. Ashridge Business School.

Huffington, A. (2015), *Thrive: The Third Metric to Redefining Success and Creating a Life of Well-Being, Wisdom and Wonder*. New York: Harmony.

Humphrey, J. (2015), *Taking the Stage: How Women can Speak Up, Stand Out and Succeed*. San Francisco: Jossey-Bass.

Ibarra, H., Carter, N. M. and Silva, C. (2010), Why Men Still Get More Promotions than Women. *Harvard Business Review* 88 (9): 80–5.

Ibarra, H., Ely, R. and Kolb, D. (2013), Women Rising: The Unseen Barriers. *Harvard Business Review* 91 (9): 60–6.

Institute of Leadership and Management (2011), *Ambition and Gender at Work*. Institute of Leadership and Management (available online at www.i-l-m.com).

Kay, K. and Shipman, C. (2015), *The Confidence Code: The Science and Art of Self-Assurance – What Women Should Know*. London: Harper Business.

Kellaway, L. (2007), *The Answers: All the Office Questions You Never Dared to Ask*. London: Profile Books.

Landel, M. (2015), Gender Balance and the Link to Performance. *McKinsey Quarterly*, February.

McKinsey & Co. (2014), *Moving Mindsets on Gender Diversity*. McKinsey Global Survey Results.

Mrs Moneypenny (Heather McGregor) (2013), *Mrs Moneypenny's Careers Advice for Ambitious Women*. London: Penguin.

Opportunity Now (2014), *Project 28–40: The Report*. Business in the Community.

O'Reilly, N. D. (2015), *Leading Women: 20 Influential Women Share Their Secrets to Leadership, Business and Life*. Avon, MA: Adams Media.

Osborne, C. (2002), *Dealing with Difficult People*. London: Dorling Kindersley.

Owen, J. (2014), *The Leadership Skills Handbook: 50 Essential Skills You Need to Be a Leader*. London: Kogan Page.

Pollitt, A. (2006), *Women Who Changed the World: Fifty Inspirational Women Who Shaped History*. London: Quercus.

Russell-Jones, N. and Hailstone, P. (2000), *The Decision-Making Pocketbook*. Alresford: Management Pocketbooks.

Sandberg, S. (2015), *Lean In: Women, Work and the Will to Lead*. London: W. H. Allen.

Schein, E. (1990), *Career Anchors (Discovering Your Real Values)*. San Francisco: Jossey-Bass Pfeiffer.

Slaughter, A. -M. (2015), *Unfinished Business: Women, Men, Work, Family*. London: Random House.

Stone, D., Patton, B. and Heen, S. (2011), *Difficult Conversations: How to Discuss What Really Matters*. London: Penguin.

Syed, M. (2010), *Bounce: How Champions Are Made*. London: Fourth Estate.

Webb, L. (2013), *Resilience: How to Cope When Everything around You Keeps Changing*. Chichester: John Wiley and Sons.

Whittell, G. (2008), *Spitfire Women of World War II*. London: HarperCollins.

Wittenberg-Cox, A. (2014), Stop Trying to Fix Women. *Talent Quarterly* 1 (3): 1.

Woman and Home Magazine. Helen Mirren: I'm still learning lessons in life; Nicola Benedetti: My best advice ever, October 2015.

Yousafzai, M. and Lamb, C. (2013), *I Am Malala: The Girl Who Stood Up for Education and Was Shot by the Taliban*. London: Weidenfeld & Nicolson Ltd.

Index